Mr. Chilehead
ADVENTURES IN THE TASTE OF PAIN

JAMES D. CAMPBELL

Other books by James D. Campbell
published by ECW Press:

Depth Markers: Selected Art Writings 1985–1994

After Geometry: The Abstract Art of Claude Tousignant

*The Thought From Outside:
The Art and Artefacts of John Heward*

For S.A.B.
Whose wayward heart knows why

and

In loving memory of Miranda
Kwan Yin Bodhisattva

Copyright © ECW PRESS, 2003

Published by ECW PRESS
2120 Queen Street East, Suite 200, Toronto, Ontario, Canada M4E 1E2

All rights reserved. No part of this publication may be reproduced,
stored in a retrieval system, or transmitted in any form by any process —
electronic, mechanical, photocopying, recording, or otherwise — without
the prior written permission of the copyright owners and ECW PRESS.

NATIONAL LIBRARY OF CANADA CATALOGUING IN PUBLICATION DATA

Campbell, James D., 1956-
Mr. Chilehead: adventures in the taste of pain/James D. Campbell
ISBN 1-55022-559-6
1. Hot pepper sauces 2. Cookery (Hot pepper sauces) I. Title.
TX819.H66C34 2003   641.3'384   C2002-905426-5

Acquisition editor: Robert Lecker. Copy editor: Mary Williams
Design & typesetting: Guylaine Régimbald — Solo Design
Production: Emma McKay. Printing: Transcontinental
Cover design: David Drummond
Back cover & endpapers painting: Stéphanie Bush

Diligent efforts have been made to contact copyright holders; please
excuse any inadvertent errors or omissions, but if anyone has been
unintentionally omitted, the publisher would be pleased to receive
notification and make acknowledgements in future printings.

Dave DeWitt's chile pepper historical research drawn
upon with kind permission.

This book is set in Bembo and ParmaPetit

The publication of *Mr. Chilehead* has been generously supported by the
Canada Council, by the Government of Ontario through the Ontario Media
Development Corporation's Ontario Book Initiative, by the Ontario Arts
Council, and by the Government of Canada through the Book Publishing
Industry Development Program. **Canadä**

DISTRIBUTION

CANADA: Jaguar Book Group, 100 Armstrong Avenue,
Georgetown, Ontario L7G 5S4

UNITED STATES: Independent Publishers Group,
814 North Franklin Street, Chicago, Illinois 60610

EUROPE: Turnaround Publisher Services, Unit 3, Olympia Trading Estate,
Coburg Road, Wood Green, London N2Z 6T2

Australia and New Zealand: Wakefield Press, 1 The Parade West
(Box 2266), Kent Town, South Australia 5071

PRINTED AND BOUND IN CANADA

ECW PRESS
ecwpress.com

Contents

Preface and Acknowledgments ... 9
Introduction: The Taste of Pain ... 11

1 Genesis of a Chilehead ... 21

2 Short Takes on the Saga of the Chile Pepper ... 31

3 Howdy, Ms. Habañero!
(aka Mademoiselle Hellfire) ... 39

4 Condiment Magma Made
and Marketed in America ... 49

5 Dave's Insanity: An Evangelical
Hot-Sauce Maker's Jihad ... 61

6 Fragments of Agony and Ecstasy:
Some Painful and Pleasurable Moments
Painfully and Pleasurably Remembered ... 73

7 Sauce-Assisted Suicide ... 109

8 Mr. Chilehead's Factual Chile Fixins:
A Chilehead-Size Helping of Not-
So-Trivial Chile Trivia ... 121

9 Erotomania in Painland: Sauce Sanctuary
for the Sex-Crazed and Politically Incorrect ... 131

Conclusion: A Short Meditation on
Hellfire and Damnation ... 144

Appendices

1	The Chile Pepper Institute	150
2	The Inexperienced Chile Taster	152
3	Mirror, Mirror on the Wall, What Are Mr. Chilehead's Picks for the Hottest Sauces of Them All?	157
4	Wilbur Scoville's Painland Scale	161
5	You Know You're a Chilehead If . . .	163
6	Mr. Chilehead's Web Sites That Matter	183
7	Mr. Chilehead's Favorite Recipes	201
	References	221

Preface and Acknowledgments

A few months after I had dutifully submitted the manuscript of this book to my publisher, I found myself at a lovely little Italian restaurant, Il Piatto Della Nonna, on rue St. Viateur in Montreal. My guests were two important Montreal-based artists: John Heward, a senior artist on whom I'd written a few books; and Yechel Gagnon, a talented younger artist whose work I hoped soon to be curating. After we'd ordered our pasta, our big-hearted hostess, Rosie Scalia, appeared unsolicited with a deep dish of pepper purée. It was a wonderful hot sauce, made in-house (with olive oil, garlic, a touch of fresh basil, fresh jalapeño peppers, and red peppers). It was nothing short of exquisite. Rosie informed me that the restaurant had been serving the sauce to legions of fortunate diners for five years. The previous night, I'd dined at one of my favorite Montreal haunts, The Mess Hall, in Westmount. I'd asked for chiles, and they served me their own homegrown mash! The waiter told me that the restaurant had started growing chiles in-house.

I mention these incidents here because they demonstrate just how popular hot sauce has become. These days, chiles wink at you from every nook and cranny—

and you'd better wink back! In the old days, anyone requesting chiles in a restaurant would have been offered crushed red chile-pepper flakes, nothing tastier or more exotic. But times have changed, and they're still a-changing as far as the hellish-hot and heaven-sent chile pepper is concerned. The geography of Painland is no doubt expanding at breakneck (or break-palate?) speed, even as Mr. Chilehead writes these words. The cartographers of culinary excess have their work cut out for them.

I would like to thank my publisher, Robert Lecker, for seeing the necessity, and perhaps the poetry, in publishing Mr. Chilehead's own funky chile-pepper love song. Mary Williams, my editor, once again restored a bedridden text to something ambulatory that I could be proud of.

I also want to thank my buddy G. Grant Lane, aka PyroMan, for all of his invaluable help along the way. He is a true savant.

To all those lovely women—muses, amanuenses, and paramedics-in-waiting—who fearlessly accompanied me to Painland before their passports had been properly stamped at the border, I extend my heartfelt thanks. And, finally, Mr. Chilehead wishes to express to you, his gentle readers—chileheads, cattle, wannabes, and hangers-on alike—his fervent hope that visions of incandescent chile peppers dance forever in your heads.

James D. Campbell
Montreal, February 2003

Introduction
The Taste of Pain

Chronic pain may be generally described as any persisting pain that occurs beyond the usual course of a disease or beyond the reasonable time for an injury to heal. Chronic chile pepper pain may be generally described as a pain that persists only as long as chile peppers are being ingested, i.e., all the time.

Chronic pain negatively impacts all aspects of an individual's life, including emotional, vocational, financial, and social elements. Chronic chile pepper pain positively impacts all aspects of an individual's life, including olfactory, emotional, sexual, vocational, financial, and social elements.

ANONYMOUS CHILEHEAD, "NO PAIN, NO GAIN"

Pain has a taste. To those of you unfamiliar with red-hot chile peppers (the fruit, that is, not the band), this might seem an absurd and, at best, unsubstantiated claim. I feel sorry for you. You probably find the notion that pain has a taste offensive. Or just plain weird. But ask yourselves this: What if pain has a taste that is not only hellishly good punishment, but also addictive, pleasurable, and even orgasmic? And you don't have to be into S&M to enjoy it. (Well, it may actually help if you are, because your pain threshold will already be way up there, and those scars on your backside will be matched by new ones inside your rectum.) For dyed-in-the-wool fans, the idea that pain has a taste is a truism. A no-brainer.

I have tasted pain. I have subjected myself to it, endured and managed it thousands upon thousands of times over the years, both at home and abroad. Why? The pain is a baptism-by-fire culinary exercise, a clear challenge not only to the taste buds, but also to our idea of fortitude—and, for that matter, any notion of human finitude. It is an endurance contest, and the knowledge of one's own limits is the prize. Just how much can you take? Will you win the contest, or are you a pathetic wuss? As chileheads say, "No pain, no gain."

The world over, peppers are used in a plethora of ways, and they have been for hundreds of years. The sheer variety of types and diversity of preparations beggar description. Peppers are an exotic aspect of the pantry, and chileheads savor them in private the way others savor pornography or handguns. Peppers are a rubric under which curry powder, cayenne pepper, red pepper, crushed red pepper, dried whole peppers, fresh whole peppers, chile powder, paprika, pickled and processed products, pimento, salsa picante, and pepper sauce can be happily subsumed. All of these forms concern us here, but our main preoccupation will be the fresh red-hot chile pepper and the hot sauces it infuses.

The sauce is life for chileheads everywhere. It's the rejuvenating waters of Painland. The offering that sets the captives free—like the blood of Christ, as we were taught in Sunday school. Hot sauce liberates us from deathly mediocre cuisine. It's all good clean fun, like creative bloodletting and medical electricity used to be; whereas the bourgeoisie of the nineteenth century had to rely on lancets and leeches to purge their bad blood and the old shock box to tone their psyches, today we can count on the chile pepper. It tickles the palate, cracks the whip on exposed flesh, and bevels the sharp edges off neuroses.

Fresh habañero, jalapeño, cayenne, and a host of other peppers always fill a large Chinese agate bowl on my kitchen table. Their bright greens, reds, and yellows are a voluptuous delight to the eye. They are a seduction, a promise of redemption, pain, pleasure—the whole damn thing. But their beauty is really internal. As the painter Paul Cézanne once said, "Nature is on the inside."

Peppers promise to liven up any dish, so the chilehead's next meal holds the expectation of heat and nirvana and paradisiacal fervor and more and more heat. Ever tried a medium-rare flank steak with sliced jalapeños, topped with habañero pepper flakes, and habañero relish on the side? It can let a little blood. Watch you don't bite your tongue when your mouth fires up! Swirl the oily heat around in your mouth—it's like some lovely Tantric effluvium from the feet of the goddess herself. The fresh peppers are extraordinarily flavorful.

From the palate through to the groin, they work their sultry magick. But when it comes to gauging the true taste of pain, bottled hot sauces are undeniably your best option. Try one and savor the pain in all its sultry, sublime, and variegated glory.

There are now so many hot-sauce makers and so many versions of the stuff out there that it numbs the brain, if not the palate. But my palate is a seasoned veteran, and my adventures in the taste of pain are ongoing. Truly, one never becomes bored by hot peppers. They exist in nature in such diversity, and they exist in sauce form in such unlikely combinations and at such heat magnitudes, that they never cease to delight—and ignite—the senses.

Hot sauce is a more-or-less liquid admixture of chiles and other substances. Sundry fruits, vegetables, herbs, and spices are blended with peppers to produce sauces that bleed flavor and ache with pain. Some sauces are so thick you have to eat them with a fork; some flow from the bottle with agonizing slowness (think of Satan's Blood or Bubba's Distilled Pussy Syrup), just like ketchup.

As well, hot sauce is hopelessly addictive, and the hotter it is, the more satisfying it can be. As the pain quotient spikes, so too does the chilehead's need to partake once again. In this sense, hot sauce is like an opiate. But this opiate has one helluva Janus-faced sting. The damage done? Unlike that of the needle, it is only temporary. Sometimes fleeting. Sometimes not fleeting enough.

The chilehead is after that quantum high, that dark and exhilarating endorphin rush that transports him or her from the mediocrity of the here and now to an ultra-heated *elsewhere*. To Painland, I mean, and points beyond—the ER, if you're careless with the dosage. But after the first deep burn of the habañero, a nirvana-like state quickly sets in, and then you'll find yourself in ardent pursuit of your next hit. Life in Hot Sauce Land—or Painland, as I choose to call it in this book—is like life in New York City's old 42nd Street environs, as described by Levon Helm in Martin Scorsese's *The Last Waltz*: "You just go in for the first time and you get your ass kicked, you take off, and as soon as it heals up you come back and you try it again. Eventually, you fall right in love with it." It offers plenty of flavor and the bracing prospect of volumetric pain. It can also be a literal pain in the ass. The best sauce burns twice, you see.

The cheerful obscenity of some hot-sauce labels—and many are completely over-the-top in their gleeful vulgarity—makes the stuff seem like forbidden fruit plucked from the Tree of Life (see chapter 9, "Erotomania in Painland"). There is even a sauce called Eve, which comes in a bottle shaped like a voluptuous woman. Think of vernal gardens hung with fruit and rife with stinging serpents. Think of Adam, his temperature and his appendage(s) rising as he reaches for that fruit. Let your eye linger lovingly over Hot Bitch at the Beach, Ultimate Burn, and legions of others whose labels are adorned with naked come-hither mamas. Take in the Ain't Milk bottle, which sports a smiling Monica wearing a white "ain't milk" mustache; the implication, of course, is that Slick Willie, his zipper down and his own red-hot chile pepper at half-mast, isn't far away. And these are just the tamer ones. Wow!

But what you see is really what you get. I just bought a bottle of Black Widow. A fearsome 3-D spider clings to its neck, and a red hourglass sits on its belly—the sinister aegis under which this most painful of sauces delivers its venomous bite to the back of the tongue. And what about The Source? At 7.1 million Scoville units (the official unit of measurement for chile-pepper heat; see appendix 4), the invitation it offers is clear: partake and expectorate or die. Got sinus problems? Erectile dysfunction? Are you frigid? A bed-wetter? The Source is your surefire (pardon the pun) cure. But remember that peppers are nightshades. The fiery chemical capsaicin in the lining of the pods exudes an oil or resin that takes no prisoners on the short trip to Painland. From the roof of the mouth to the root of the tongue, this oil is like a living flame that leaves only cinders and traumatized sphincters in its wake. The sauces that contain the distillate of this oil are painfully pleasurable.

Hot sauce has been consumed for millennia, but these days it's ubiquitous. It has become as much a part of patented Americana as the apple pie. The sauce appeals to individualists, creative personalities, and raunchy gourmands everywhere, but in America it has become the focus of a thriving subculture (see chapter 4, "Condiment Magma Made and Marketed in America"). What is it about Americans, anyway? All over the U.S., people who appear sane and orderly by day become sauce alchemists by night. In their quest to discover the philosopher's stone of Painland, they distill their own kinky brands of the sauce in labs they've rigged up in the basements of their homes. Their almighty unholy grail is the ultimate hot sauce, a brew that's akin to liquid gold, the stuff that removes the lining of your mouth while delivering flavor full force. Those who ingest this substance may wind up in hospital, but at least they get the lick they're after. I'm talking about sauces like Bad Day in Baghdad, Satan's Blood, Smack My Ass and Call Me Sally: Chet's Gone Mad, and Dave's Da' Bomb: The Final Answer, to name but a few.

More recently, with the tremendous proliferation of commercially produced hot sauces, these comestibles have become eminently collectible. Specialty sauces have grabbed upwards of 25 percent of the U.S. condiment market. It's no surprise, really. Once word of the painful pleasure of the sauce had spread, there was no stopping it. It's as if certain driven, courageous, or just plain foolhardy inheritors of America's old pioneering spirit have turned hot sauce Painland into a kind of culinary Wild West (or, better yet, a culinary Gold Rush). Perhaps these individuals have understood that the athleticism of a palate taunted and engaged is a lovely thing to behold, that the ingenious and purely instinctive calisthenics involved boggle the mind.

The fanaticism of hot-sauce collectors is beyond the pale. More than 2,000 different hot sauces line my pantry shelves, and that just isn't enough. I am always searching for new ones. If I taste something and find that it delivers the pain and the flavor, I savor the scorpion sting for a moment and then order 50 bottles. I am a hoarder of hot sauces. I have resorted to buying entire collections from others in order to expand my own. I recently saw a bottle of Blair's 5 a.m. (1.5 million Scoville units) for sale on eBay with a $600 reserve. Did the buyer actually open the bottle? Only the Shadow knows ... or perhaps the undertaker. Seen the cult horror film *Phantasm/Oblivion*? I can picture the Tall Man decanting the stuff as a means of drawing the innocent into his mausoleum morgue opening upon Avernus.

We chileheads crave hotter and hotter sauces. Why? We get a wee bit jaded, is all. Pain is addictive, and one does need to increase one's dosage in order to see things straight. Some sauces are so hot that you have to sign legal waivers in order to obtain them. Dave's Ultimate Insanity Limited Edition comes in its own wooden casket, and the yellow caution labels it bears are quite explicit (as they should be). Open at your own risk. This is one dangerous sauce!

Hot sauce is a test of one's stamina—or one's manhood, perhaps? And yet, while most hot-sauce manufacturers are men, as many women as men are dyed-in-the-sauce fanatics. They carry bottles of the stuff around in their purses and throw hot-sauce parties in their homes—a welcome alternative to the old-fashioned Tupperware party. Women rule in Painland, and they can set terrible challenges.

Are you a wussy boy? Not sure? Well, you can find out easily enough in Painland. Just let a Red Queen palpate your tongue, or gulp down Dave's Insanity like root beer and hang in there while an excruciating burning sensation in your nether region keeps you glued to a seat in the smallest room in the house. The question you must ask yourself when confronted with a truly hot sauce is this: Do I feel lucky? Well, do you, sucker? And when you're on the floor, hyperventilating, experiencing that sweet cardiac arrhythmia brought on by the incendiary heat, don't be surprised if it feels as though your heart has been touched not by Dirty Harry but by Christ. (Or perhaps that fellow down below is playing Pin the Tail on the Piñata with your organ, piercing it with his pitchfork, once, twice, three times for good measure).

Think of the book you are now holding in your hands as a travel guide to Painland, that strangest of culinary geographies. On our brief journey, I will assume the role of amateur ethnographer. I hope to shed some light on the strange subculture of my fellow chileheads, to show you the true shape of our desires, and if I should convert some unbelievers or just plain innocent bystanders along the scorched pepperway, I believe that my efforts will have been well worth it. For the more chileheads there are in this world, the closer we'll all be to heaven and hell, and the healthier and happier and more hospitable life on this planet will become.

I, Mr. James D. Chilehead, will now lead you on a search for the truth about hot sauce, which some hold to be the proverbial elixir of life. Let us all celebrate its divine efflorescence! Keep this book under lock and key in your pantry. Like Burton's *Arabian Nights*, it might be considered a subversive tome. Remember, gentle readers, there are unseen precipices herein! Proceed with caution. Take everything you read here with a prophylactic grain of salt—or, better yet, a teaspoon of Dave's Ultimate Insanity Special Reserve. But once you catch fire, don't complain to Mr. Chilehead, you hear? Keep your fire extinguisher close at hand. Enjoy a good roasting on your own culinary pyre, and savor your spontaneous combustions when and if you can. As your teeth clench and your tongue withers, as your parched lips crack open and your teeth sizzle, as the roof of your mouth fissures and your vocal chords dissolve, as the smoke rises slowly, ever so slowly, from your esophagus and that other opening further down, heed my words: Taste the pain.

1
Genesis of a Chilehead

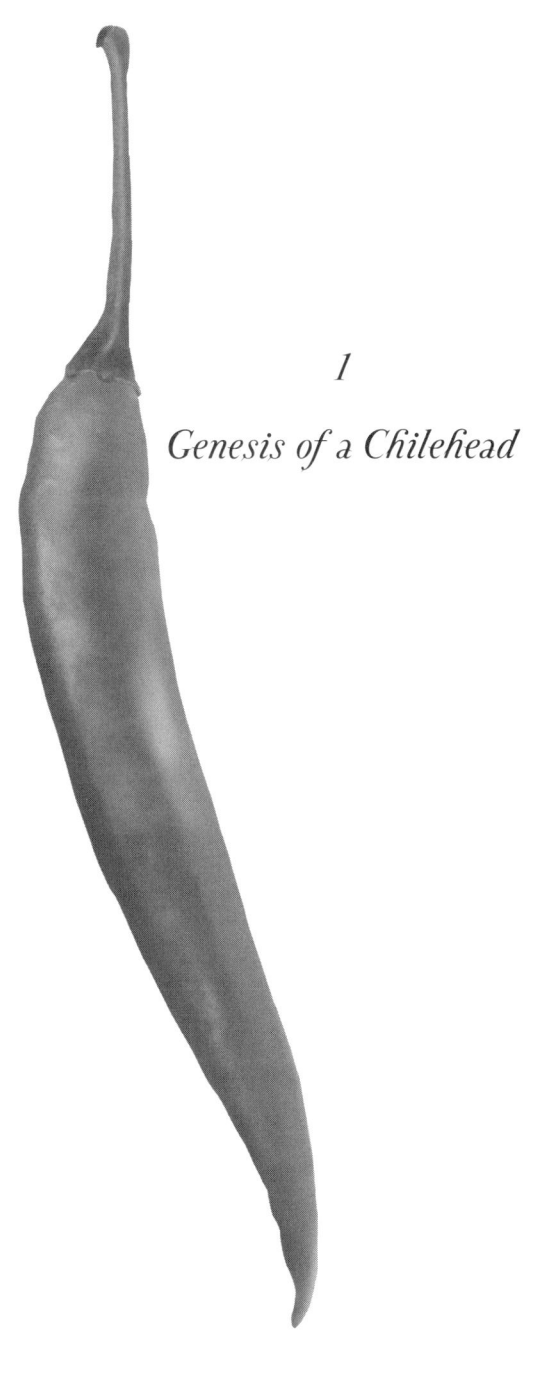

> *All true chileheads have been baptized*
> *in fire, not water.*
> ANONYMOUS CHILEHEAD

When I was still but a wee child, my father, an unrepentant Scot in every other respect, imported the tropics into our home via the pantry. The aromas of cumin, turmeric, and chile powder were pervasive. The pie safe harbored no pies. Only fresh peppers. A lovely, dense odor rose from it, which, in the summer heat, would saturate the pantry air. At age six, I would play doctor with the little girl from next door under the heady mistletoe of that scent.

My father's yen for culinary heat led our family far afield: we abandoned homeland haggis, weak-kneed porridge, and Highland scones. Instead of cod liver oil, we dosed ourselves with the cure-all pepper pod. My father devised a killer spaghetti sauce that endeared him to the local Italian community. The recipe was remarkable in that it called for liberal quantities of cumin, turmeric, curry powder, and red-hot chile peppers. Needless to say, the sauce had heat, but it was not overwhelmingly hot. However, from time to time, after a few drams of the good old mountain dew on a Sunday afternoon, my father would mistakenly add two or three times the normal amount of spice. This was never a problem for me. It only amounted to a more exotic experience for my increasingly well-seasoned palate.

My youth was brightened by that spaghetti sauce. It was, to put it simply, extraordinarily good. I am now in sole possession of the recipe, and I make a batch several times a year, adding a little fresh habañero pepper to spike the heat quotient. I freeze the sauce, and then I can enjoy my fiery stash whenever the mood strikes. As a gift to chileheads everywhere, I have included the recipe in appendix 7, "Mr. Chilehead's Favorite Recipes."

One evening when I was about 20, I visited a tiny Montreal souvlaki joint, where I'd become a regular. On that occasion, I requested and was served a wicked hot sauce on my souvlaki pita. It was inordinately flavorful. Suddenly, I was hooked. My palate did an elephantine pirouette. I had to have more of that lovely, silken fire that smote my mouth with raw desire. I asked the chef for the recipe, and he confessed that it came from a bottle. Still, it was ferociously good—and hotter (in the culinary realm, that is) than anything I had ever experienced. The chef added that he'd received raves about the sauce from many of his customers. He also said that he'd instructed the staff to warn those who ordered the sauce about its effects. The fiery substance was a Jamaican import, and the chef mentioned that I could buy it at a nearby Jamaican market. I purchased close to 200 bottles because I'd developed a powerful instantaneous crush on it. Ah, first love! But all things must pass in this life. Soon enough, I needed more heat. I was starting to feel inured to the Jamaican sauce, and the prospect of hotter sauces or different sauces beckoned.

A few years later, I became an aficionado of Indian vindaloo curries, washed down with liberal amounts of on-tap British ale. But hot sauce remained a fixture in my pantry. That was 25 years ago. I was a late-blooming chilehead, perhaps, yet I rode the crest of the heat wave as the hot sauce came on. I now have a vast collection of hot sauces from all over the world. While I'm sorry to say that there are still thousands more I lack, I tell myself that there's always tomorrow.

True chileheads may be born (if you have a hypertrophied palate, that is), not bred, but those formative experiences certainly made me a heat seeker, a devotee of the spice, a pepper slave, a hotfooted knave. They also lured me into a series of pain-tasting adventures. I became a chilehead because of the promise of heat and flavor and, yes, sublime interior punishment. Chileheads cherish colorful exotica. In a multicultural society, we are paragons of experimentalism and openness.

We are philoxenes, not xenophobes, you hear? All that redneck nonsense that you find in Painland is just there to piss off the politically correct. Political correctness can be the bane of all freethinking people everywhere, and Chileheads in particular, as I am reminded when I listen to a certain anthem—call it a clarion call —by the inimitable John Mellencamp. I refer to his "Peaceful World" wherein he names the hypocrisy that has crippled our culture. Well, Chileheads saw through it all from the outset, and eviscerated it with a vengeance, too. Listen to Mellencamp (though many of you probably already know the lyrics), and be converted.

Hypocrite? Poseur? Neurasthenic? Uptight? Tight-assed? Got some issues with freedom of expression? Better steer clear of Painland, then. It's not that you're not wanted. It's just that it may be far more than you can handle, sugar. Anyhow, you've been warned. At the Painland border, there's a huge hoarding constructed of billions of chile peppers—serrano, jalapeño, habañero, chipotle, cayenne, and many others—and on it, in blazing letters, are the words "Everyone Welcome." In smaller letters, the declaration "It's Always Summer Here" appears. In still smaller letters, the following words are inscribed: "Warning. Temperature advisory: moderate to hellishly hot; bring a Tilley hat, suntan lotion, sunglasses, burn cream, milk, and plenty of cold ale. No children or pets allowed. Free admission. Free wild rides courtesy of a straitjacketed Dave H. Commentary courtesy of Dave D."

Once, I'd never leave home without hot sauce. If I did, I'd first make sure that it would be available in suitable quantities at my destination. No problem today. The sauce prevails. Chilehead culture is deeply entrenched. The religion has taken hold. Adherents are everywhere; they are poised to take over local and federal governments at all levels. Across the U.S. and Canada, thousands of worshipers gather to praise the sauce. The movement puts Billy Graham's crusade to shame. (Well, not quite—a little hyperbole is endemic to Painland, as you will discover.)

We're all evangelical. We want to rock and roll in Painland, to lock and load and do pain by the numbers, no-holds-barred. In our hectic parish, we want to convert the unbelievers and draw them into the sacred and profane pepper culture. We want them to go out and buy hot sauce bibles and memorize sauce descriptions as if they were scripture, the living word of a fire-breathing deity.

The quest for heat was accelerated when North Americans began traveling abroad in increasing numbers. They would discover new, exotic varieties of peppers and return home intent on sharing their passion with family and friends. Immigration also played a role. West Indians, for whom the condiment hot sauce has always reigned supreme, brought their culinary traditions with them to our shores. Jamaicans, Southeast Asians, and East Indians also brought with them their love of the spice. Even the Brits made a solid contribution. In the late 1960s and into the 1970s, businesses recruited skilled tradespeople from Britain. Upon arrival, the Brits found themselves in the middle of a culinary drought. It was hot food they were missing, vindaloo curries, and so they, too, added their desire for heat to the mix. All of this fueled the hot-food industry. Hallelujah for immigration! Immigration is good.

If you were to ask me what we chileheads really want, I would have to say that it is to be incinerated for our sins. This need drives us to seek out the incendiary, not the mediocrity of lukewarm spice. We want a sauce that floats on the palate like a butterfly, then stings like a bee. We want a spice that fondles the taste buds even as it flays the tongue. Come to think of it, is there a Muhammad Ali hot sauce out there? If there isn't, there should be.

We chileheads want the flash fire, but we also relish the fiery blowback. Call it "backdraft," once it works its serpentine, insidious way through the intestinal tract. We want a sauce that is hellishly hot, yes, but it must also pack a heck of a lot of flavor. There's the rub: finding a highly combustible sauce that's still succulent on the palate. A difficult equation for the manufacturers to resolve, but there are some savants out there, thank Christ! Our beloved Dave H. is one of them. His insanity is matched only by our own. And yet there are times when we want to be staggered by the heat, as it burns itself into our very souls, as it flagellates the palate and scourges the lips, tongue, throat, stomach, and, yes, anus. The truly hot sauce delivers us from the mediocrity celebrated elsewhere in our culture.

Everyone in Painland has a story worth sharing. The hot-sauce addiction always has a point of origin, a scorched ground of inception. For the doyenne of hot sauce, Jennifer Trainer Thompson, that point occurred at about the same time as my own epiphany—1980, or thereabouts. She was sailing from West Palm Beach to the British Virgin Islands when engine trouble hit. Thompson and crew were forced to disembark on a tiny island in the Bahamian chain. In need of refreshment, they went into a local eatery and ordered rum punches and French fries. Thompson proceeded to douse her fries with the contents of a recycled rum bottle full of an innocuous-looking yellow sauce. Then she wolfed down the fries. In *Hot Licks*, she describes what happened next: "Within moments I was socked with an intense pain that threatened to tear off the roof of my mouth. My com- panions—who had definitely sailed these waters before—howled with laughter as tears streamed down my cheeks, and I discovered Caribbean hot sauces and their main ingredient: the incendiary Scotch bonnet pepper... Minutes later, however, I found myself going back for more of this fiery potion. Once I had gotten past the pain, the sauce had actually tasted rather good" (1). Thompson, a remarkable proselytizer for the hot sauce cause, was baptized by fire. Just as we've all been.

When you bite into the bare habañero, that most elegant and comely of fruits, your teeth sink into liquid fire and there's no doubt that you've just partaken of the ripe, yoni-like flesh of a fire goddess —paradoxically offering you absolution through hellfire. No hair-pie here! A few seeds, maybe. The fruit is a veritable gift from the gods. Well, cruel but just, and generous gods they must be. The fruit is manna from heaven.

Surely the Mayans believe that, as custodians of the blessed habañero. And theirs is an ancient culture that was once awash in blood. In Pre-Columbian times, when a Mayan chief stood before the multitudes on the summit of a temple and sliced open his penis with an obsidian blood-letter, his ability to do so probably derived from his being a chilehead, inured to pain. What is all that talk about hallucinogens, anyway? A chile pepper will do just as well, and it won't drive you mad. Well, you may go mad from the pain, but it's transient—you'll regain your sanity soon enough.

Of course, once you take a hit of the lush and lovely habañero, you'll find it very difficult to stop there. It's very much like sex. The other ingredients in a pepper dish are like Victoria's Secret lingerie: you'll dispense with them quickly. Enough is never enough when it comes to the pepper. One hit, as any crack addict will attest, just won't do. The hot pepper is not an opiate, but it might as well be. One endorphin rush leads to another, and soon the pepper takes on a larger-than-life significance. Well, it looms large as far as food preparation is concerned. Hashish might bring on the munchies, but the pepper does, too, and it pulls no "punchies."

I remember sitting on a country-house veranda late one summer evening. The lake spread tremulously below me like a Chinese bronze mirror, reflecting a shadowy and seductive landscape. A lovely bowl of deep-green jalapeños sat on a side table. Biting into a fresh pepper, I felt the oil flow like a punitive but innocuous virus from my lips to my tongue to the roof of my mouth and points south. It was as though I'd died and gone to pepper heaven. Pretty hot for heaven, though. Again, one thinks of points south. Sometimes, points southernmost. Hindmost. Catch my meaning? The pepper will get to you. Yes, it surely will. In the end.

2

Short Takes on the Saga of the Chile Pepper

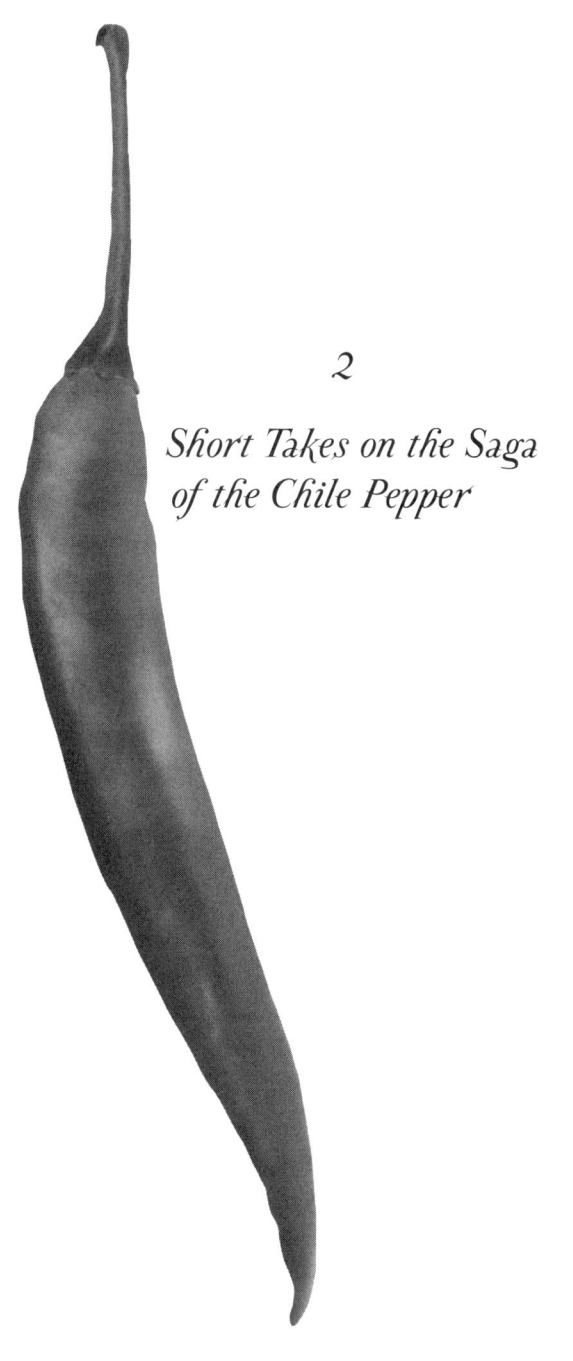

> *To the discoverer of peppers, Christopher Columbus,*
> *who may not have been the first citizen*
> *of the Old World to reach the New World but*
> *was the first to document his discoveries and to*
> *deliberately and accurately return to lay claim, thereby*
> *opening a vast new frontier that altered the world.*

JEAN ANDREWS, DEDICATION IN PEPPERS

Christopher Columbus invented hot sauce. Yes, he did. Is your eyebrow raised in skepticism? Are you shaking your head? Mute with disbelief? Well, it's a little-known historical fact that Columbus was decanting his own hotter-than-hot habañero pepper sauce while aboard the *Pinta*, or was it the *Santa Maria*? Apparently, he challenged his crew to some serious chile-tasting exercises, but the men survived. Barely. Or so I'm led to believe. Well, actually, I only have this on the authority of a fellow chilehead, so it could be apocryphal. The same chilehead (whose name I won't reveal due to pending legalities) served me Habanero 750 and told me it was Louisiana Gold, so you have to wonder. Being a chilehead does not automatically confer virtue. It might even be a mandate for mischief. But I digress.

In any case, the saga of the chile pepper began with Columbus. Of course, where it really started is a matter of far-from-idle speculation; its origins are, sadly, not a part of recorded history. If the site of the world's first pepper tree could be pinpointed, that site would become a venerable destination for countless earnest chilehead pilgrims. It would become the chilehead Fountain of Youth, the church of our nativity, so to speak. On that holy shrine, we chileheads would converge to scatter habañero seeds like latter-day Johnny Pepperseeds.

Columbus traveled to the New World with the purpose of scoring black pepper, which was adored and jealously hoarded back home. The pepper he found was not exactly the pepper he'd envisioned, but our beloved hot sauce was the fruit of his ambition and his discerning palate. So, the desire for new sources of black pepper was a main motivation for Columbus's 1492 voyage, but his serendipitous discovery of the chile pepper became the fulcrum that culinary adventurers would use to attain exoticism and sophistication and undreamed-of heat. A dietary staple of the New World Indians, the chile soon upped the ante of Old World cuisine.

Yes. Columbus, discoverer of peppers, invented hot sauce. Was he himself a dyed-in-the-sauce devotee? Very probably. Did he bottle and market his own "I Am the Discoverer/Chilehead Emeritus" hot sauce? Probably not. He died in obscurity in 1506. Was Columbus the original chilehead? Impossible to say. For all we know, that honor belongs to someone who lived much earlier on the timeline—a Neanderthal, perhaps. But Columbus's name will always enjoy the premier spot in the Hot Sauce Hall of Flame.

In a letter to Ferdinand and Isabella and the treasurer of Aragon, Columbus made reference to his discovery: "In these islands there are mountains where the cold this winter was very severe, but the people endure it from habit, and with the aid of the meat they eat with *very hot spices*" (quoted in Andrews, 102–3, italics added). The pungent berries—those "very hot spices"—they used to season their food were reminiscent of black peppercorns, and so the explorer was convinced that he'd discovered a new type of black pepper. He hadn't, of course. What Columbus had stumbled upon was the habañero, known to the indigenous population as "aji."

On a subsequent voyage, Columbus took along a noted scholar and physician named Diego Alvarez Chanca. Dr. Chanca is credited with having produced the first written account of the West Indian chile pepper. In discussing the indigenous diet, he explained that the island people seasoned their food with "a vegetable called *agé*." They used it "to give a sharp taste to the fish and such birds as they can catch, of the infinite variety there are in this island, dishes of which they prepare in different ways" (qtd. in Andrews, 3).

Columbus transported bushels of peppers and allspice back to the Iberian Peninsula and the Atlantic Islands, where their reputation as culinary enhancers had quickly spread. Known to the Europeans as "pimiento," the chile pepper was revered, and it rapidly began its global circuit. Everywhere it went, it attracted devotees—chile-pepper aficionados, chileheads before that appellation was ever invented. Its obsessives. Its marketers, its manufacturers, its masters of mayhem, mischief, and self-immolation. The pepper pervaded some Chinese cuisines, and it infiltrated Indian cuisine so thoroughly that before long it was commonly supposed to have originated in India. But the best evidence suggests that it originated in South America—perhaps in Bolivia, in the dense Amazon jungle. But no one knows for sure.

Chile peppers have moved effortlessly across geographic, psychological, and culinary boundaries. Over 200 varieties have been identified. Plant geneticists have gotten in on Mother Nature's act and are developing more all the time. And who can say what species remain undiscovered in the least accessible regions of Mexico and South America? Somewhere there may even be a chile pepper far hotter than the habañero. A lethal, primeval, hotter-than-our-sun's-core chile pepper that will set this world and the imaginations of its inhabitants on fire. Well, one can dream.

Chile plants, like rabbits and the Irish, are very prolific, so watch out! Some cross-pollinate feverishly, and this could yield fiery results—or some disappointingly mild ones. Keep your plants separate, under lock and key, so they can't jump one another's bones. Catch them in flagrante delicto, and the voyeur in you may be in for the hottest and most sweat-drenched thrashing of his/her dwee lifetime. Best to leave them to their own devices until you have cause to use them. Wear gloves! A blind chilehead with a bad rash on hands and face is not who you want to be.

Chiles have several incarnations. You can buy them fresh, frozen, powdered, or canned. Each incarnation has its own uses. Fresh is always best. Fresh chiles will last a few weeks in the fridge wrapped in paper towels. If you consume a lot of them, store them in your pantry. Canned chiles can be problematic, because they tend to have a metallic flavor; the exceptions are chipotles in adobo sauce or pickled chipotles. Many supermarkets now carry jalapeños, and some stock habañeros and scotch bonnets as well.

All over the world, the chile pepper is revered as the spice queen of culinary heaven. When the pepper hit Thailand, the population went wild. The Thais consume more hot peppers than any other people on the planet: an average of five grams of hot peppers per person, per day. The East Indians are close behind them (what chilehead of any consequence is not a vindaloo addict)? The Koreans are also notable consumers. Kimchi, a lovely staple of Korean cuisine, is strongly spiced with dried red pepper. But any cuisine can be rehabilitated by the chile pepper. Transformed. Enhanced.

More recently, of course, the chile pepper has sparked and stoked a feeding frenzy in the U.S. (see chapter 4). In America, the pepper has redeemed a dead-palate population. Multitudes have been entranced by rumors of damnation—which human flesh, according to the Scriptures, should be unable to endure. Dead-palates are being reborn as firecrackers as the oversalted food of yesterday morphs into the searing ambrosia of today— and the day after. If you occasionally detect the stench of sulfur in the air, there's a good reason for it: the closer you get to heaven, the more closely the atmosphere resembles that of the other place down below.

Seriously, though, chile peppers open a window on the infinite. They offer culinary salvation and an idyll of togetherness. Not for nothing do people say, "The family that sautées chiles together, stays together."

Encountering a habañero in the course of eating can be as instantly civilizing as hearing a strain of Bach. Divorce in the works? Go shopping for habañeros! Serve them to your spouse, and you may rekindle some real warmth. Trouble with the boss? Present him/her with a bottle of Vicious Viper. Advise him/her to partake of it liberally. Trouble in the bedroom? Surreptitiously slip a few a few drops of Satan's Blood into your partner's Bloody Mary—it just might do the trick. But do not—and I repeat, do not—use Pure Cap extract on the privates to harden things up. Believe me, you don't want to go there. And don't add it to the massage oil, either, or you'll be racing from the bedroom to the burn ward.

If, as some commentators tell us, almost three-quarters of the world's population regularly consumes chiles, no wonder the global climate is warming. And in that warm atmosphere, chiles are bringing people together. Chileheads compare notes, swap anecdotes, witness each other's acts of bravura (or acts of temporary mental retardation, depending on how you look at it); they meet to exchange burn cream recommendations, guzzle beer or milk, and so forth.

Savant and dear sister in pepperdom Jean Andrews has noted that the earliest known record of the pepper comes from Tehuacán, some 150 miles south of Mexico City. Analysis of seeds and fossilized human feces found in and around the ancient cave dwellings there has determined that the cave-dwellers were consuming peppers as early as 7000 B.C. Somewhere between 5200 and 3400 B.C., they were cultivating them. Pepper plants were among the first—along with bean, corn, and squash plants—to be domesticated in the Americas.

For at least 9,000 years, chileheads have flourished on Spaceship Earth. What a glorious and ultraheated human epic is the ongoing saga of the chile pepper!

3

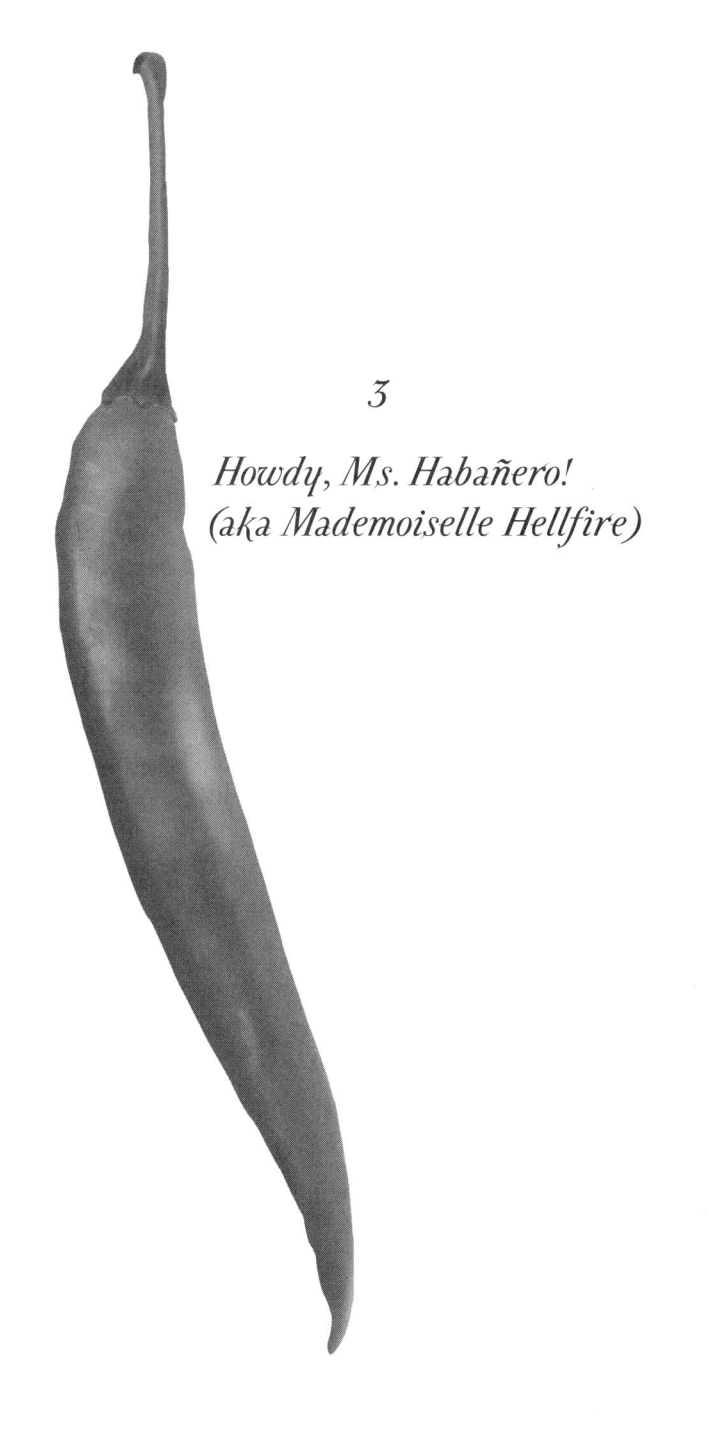

*Howdy, Ms. Habañero!
(aka Mademoiselle Hellfire)*

> *Without the habañero, we might just as*
> *well be dead in the water.*
> ANONYMOUS CHILEHEAD

> *Dead cattle in the water.*
> ANOTHER ANONYMOUS CHILEHEAD, AS A QUALIFICATION

Now, you may ask Mr. Chilehead this question out of sublime ignorance, and thus endear yourself to him: What is a habañero? A Cuban formal dance routine? A kind of Mexican cowboy hat? You've missed the boat by the moon and all the outer darkness besides, my friend.

The species name, *capsicum chinense jacquin,* doesn't tell you much. In fact, all you need to know about the habañero is what it does to the inside of your mouth, your taste buds, and the lining of your anus (the alkaloid capsaicin does not break down in the digestive process, so when you excrete it, you severely "regrete" it). As Jean Andrews observes in *Peppers: The Domesticated Capsicums,* "This is the one that separates the men from the boys" (129). And the women from the girls. And the chileheads from the rest of you cattle. Don't appreciate being called cattle? Then go out and buy a habañero.

The chile pepper can be readily identified by its color, size, and shape. There is nothing lovelier in nature.

What a piece of work is a chile! Designed by the angels, surely. The habañero is a dark-green-to-orange or orange-red fruit. The fruit of fruits. The ne plus ultra of all the peppers sown and grown in Painland. It is bright red when fully ripened. It is pleasantly plump, pleasingly firm, either round or oblong, with gentle curves that remind us of the female sex organ in full flower, the beloved yoni. Habañeros are typically between one and two inches long and between one-and-one-quarter and one-and-three-quarter inches wide. If you're a true chilehead, then the moment you lay eyes on them in the market you'll experience a sexual frisson. You'll want to caress their plump smoothness, acutely aware that there's a wildfire raging inside. By the way, a wee dram of pepper vodka (steep a few habañeros in a bottle of your favorite vodka, then store the bottle in your freezer) is perhaps the finest aphrodisiac known to humankind.

Habañero literally means "from Havana," because some believed that the pepper hailed from Havana, Cuba (such great tobacco is grown there that we could make the connection and designate the habañero the Cohiba Robusto of chile peppers . . .). While this historical assertion may be true, it has been discredited by those who claim the habañero is a native of Mexico's Yucatán Peninsula. Habañeros have long been cultivated in that part of the world, and the Yucatán had extensive trade ties with Cuba until the last century. Or perhaps the habañero's true origins are in South America—some say it was incubated in the bowels of Mount Vesuvius. Others contend that habañero seeds traveled to this planet aboard a meteorite. Today, thousands of tons of habañeros are harvested every year in Mexico, Costa Rica, Texas, Belize, and California. Currently, New Mexico is at the top of the chile-producing heap, with over 21,000 acres given over to the cause.

Mexicans consume 75 percent of their country's habañero production fresh; the peppers are sliced, saturated with lime juice, and used to enhance the flavor of a range of dishes. Less than 25 percent of the crop is processed into sauces. The habañero is the holy grail of Mexico's Mayan Indians. In his admirable book *Peppers*, Amal Naj notes that the Mayans treat with disdain most other varieties of pepper. They are habañero lovers, and their devotion is bred in the bone. The jawbone, one assumes, while chewing the fruit. The habañero contains some belladonna-like alkaloids—not exactly peyote, but the living embodiment of a hallucinogenic heat.

The flavor of the habañero is highly distinctive. Words dissolve into imprecision when one attempts to express the distinctiveness of that flavor as well as its aromatic nature. Like an otherworldly opiate, it makes its presence felt, and then it can never be forgotten. Like a first love, it leaves its mark. On both the palate and the heart (and the sweat glands, of course). It hypertrophies the former and jumpstarts the latter. And it puts one in the mood for love.

The habañero is indubitably the world's most incendiary chile pepper, whether it's grown in Central America or the Caribbean or anywhere else for that matter. Now it seems that the lowly (well, I mean downright homely, at least by contrast with our beloved habañero) tepín is a rival to be reckoned with. Apparently, a scant ounce of dried tepín pods will produce a detectable hotness in 30,000 to 50,000 ounces of salsa! That's five times hotter than the orange or red habañero. The only other pepper in the world that approximates the tepín is the White Bullet habañero. (I have not tried it myself, but I am told that one can concoct the world's hottest natural hot sauce by mixing tepín pepper flakes with lime juice to taste. Let the mixture stand for 24 hours, blend, add enough additional lime juice to make a pourable sauce, and refrigerate. The sauce is rumored to last indefinitely.) The problem with the tepín is its small size. It's just plain pathetic looking. It looks more like a magnified pink pepper seed than a fruit. It lacks aesthetic appeal even if it does win the heat olympics, if you see what I mean. But that pepper is hot, so I will be cautious and diss it no further.

In Scoville units, the habañero measures anywhere between 200,000 and 300,000. This secures its position at the top of the heat scale. One of its closest relatives is the Jamaican-born and -bred Scotch bonnet, which lacks the habañero's extreme heat, piquancy, and robust aroma, but which is a perfectly adequate substitute for many recipes. Yet for those smitten with the habañero, to make such a substitution may seem like cheating on a lover. The habañero goes by a host of other names—such as congo, ginnie, and pimientia chairo—but who cares? *Habañero* suits us chileheads just fine, thanks.

So, the habañero is a highly desirable and combustible comestible. Those of us who enjoy it on a daily basis have, despite our best efforts, been burned once, twice, scores of times. And I do not mean burned voluntarily, through ingestion—I mean burned through blatant stupidity. Forgetfulness is not a trait you want to indulge around hot peppers. Touching the pepper and then touching the eyes or any other part of the body is nothing short of foolhardy, but chileheads do slip up from time to time. Remember that the taste buds can detect one-millionth of a drop of pepper juice. A couple of drops on your skin can make the worst sunburn you've ever suffered seem like a cakewalk. If you value your sight, employ extreme caution. Need to pee? For both God's sake and your own, wash your hands before unzipping your trousers. If you don't, you'll find yourself on a one-way trip to outer Painland. And you can cancel any romantic plans you may have for at least a fortnight. Unless, of course, well, you like it that way . . .

The habañero has an idyllic, exotic, islandish character. Under its influence, you can feel like Robinson Crusoe with a boner; that flavor, redolent of tropical sensuality, is nature's own erector set. The habañero is lush, luscious, lust-inducing, libidinal, lascivious. Lovely, just lovely. It induces Mr. Chilehead and others of his ilk to attempt excessive alliterative feats. It floats on the palate, slowly secreting its devilish, ineffable oil, parsing out its immolating fire. Remarkably, its liquid heat has a flavor that is somehow voluptuous and sedate—and off the scale. The good girl and the bad girl of Pepperland in a single fruit. Its flavor makes it an ideal ingredient in dishes containing tomatoes or certain tropical fruits. When ripe, the habañero can be a little sweeter and maybe a touch less potent than it is in its early green-devil incarnation.

Nowhere does the habañero express its versatility and genius better than in hot sauce. In the last dozen or so years, the variety of hot sauces containing habañero peppers has increased tremendously. Its appearance on a hot-sauce label is practically a guarantee of authenticity and big flavor. There are now well over 1,000 brands of habañero hot sauce on the U.S. market. I can safely predict that during the next decade thousands more will make their debuts. It seems that everyone wants to jump on the habañero bandwagon en route to Painland. Well, there's plenty of room.

Our adored Dave Hirschkopf has certainly played his part in bringing on this habañero madness. He's right up there with Christopher Columbus in the Hot Sauce Hall of Flame. And Dave DeWitt, spice guru, unerring savant, and Pope of Painland, is definitely at the head of the class. So is Jennifer Trainer Thompson, God bless her heart. Then there are those thousands of men and women who have challenged Mother Nature and their own pain thresholds with their homemade and often very funky habañero sauces.

I sensed that it was getting wild out there when hot-sauce producer the McIlhenny Company started using habañeros in their table sauces, and those sauces sold well. The habañero, which conventional wisdom might indicate would always be a specialty item, is catching fire and liberating taste buds across the land. Habañeros are now almost indispensable in the production of hot sauce. Up, up and away, my lovely habañero!

Each habañero hot sauce has a unique persona and market niche. Perhaps the most readily available versions are those based on fruits and vegetables. Some are tame; some are searingly hot. Some sauce manufacturers have even taken to infusing their habañero creations with liquor, such as dark rum or tequila.

While the presence of the regal habañero in a sauce is a guarantee of heat, we chileheads—demanding and discerning fanatics that we are—also crave flavor, and sauce makers compete with one another to give us both vital elements. This requires a certain ingenuity on their part. It's not so easy to balance ingredients in an admixture that tickles the palate with tendrils of fire and a taste to die for. There are the extracts, which must be used very cautiously in the preparation of a dish. There are also the purées and relishes, which consist of mashed habañeros and which may employ lime juice as a preservative (a touch of habañero purée served alongside a steak has saved many a tough, bland cut of meat from winding up in the garbage pail). Then there are the pickles—habañeros submerged in a vinegar solution. But whatever form it takes, the habañero always delivers on its promise of heat and flavor.

Hey, have I got a slow-cooker beef recipe for you! Yes, yes—I know Mr. Chilehead's favorite recipes are supposed to be relegated to the back of the book, but this is my party so I can do what I want to. Here's a gift for you, my fearless fellow chileheads. But take heed: when the dish is done and you go to lift slow-cooker lid, stand well back and do not inhale. Those vapors could fry you alive. (Are you prematurely balding, by any chance? Then hold your breath, close your eyes, and stick your head carefully into the cooker for a moment. By the next morning, who knows? You may have grown a full head of hair . . .)

Habañeroized Steak

2 pounds lean steak
4 habañeros, chopped
2 tbsp. dried minced onion
1 cup beef broth
1/4 cup soy sauce
1 tsp. garlic powder
1 tsp. turmeric

Cut steak into smallish portions. Place half the pieces in slow cooker, and lay the habañeros on top. Layer remaining steak pieces on top of the habañeros. Mix remaining ingredients together and pour over meat. Cover and cook on low setting for 8 to 10 hours, or on high for 4 to 5 hours (slow is better). Season with habañero pepper flakes to taste, and serve. Serves 6.

4

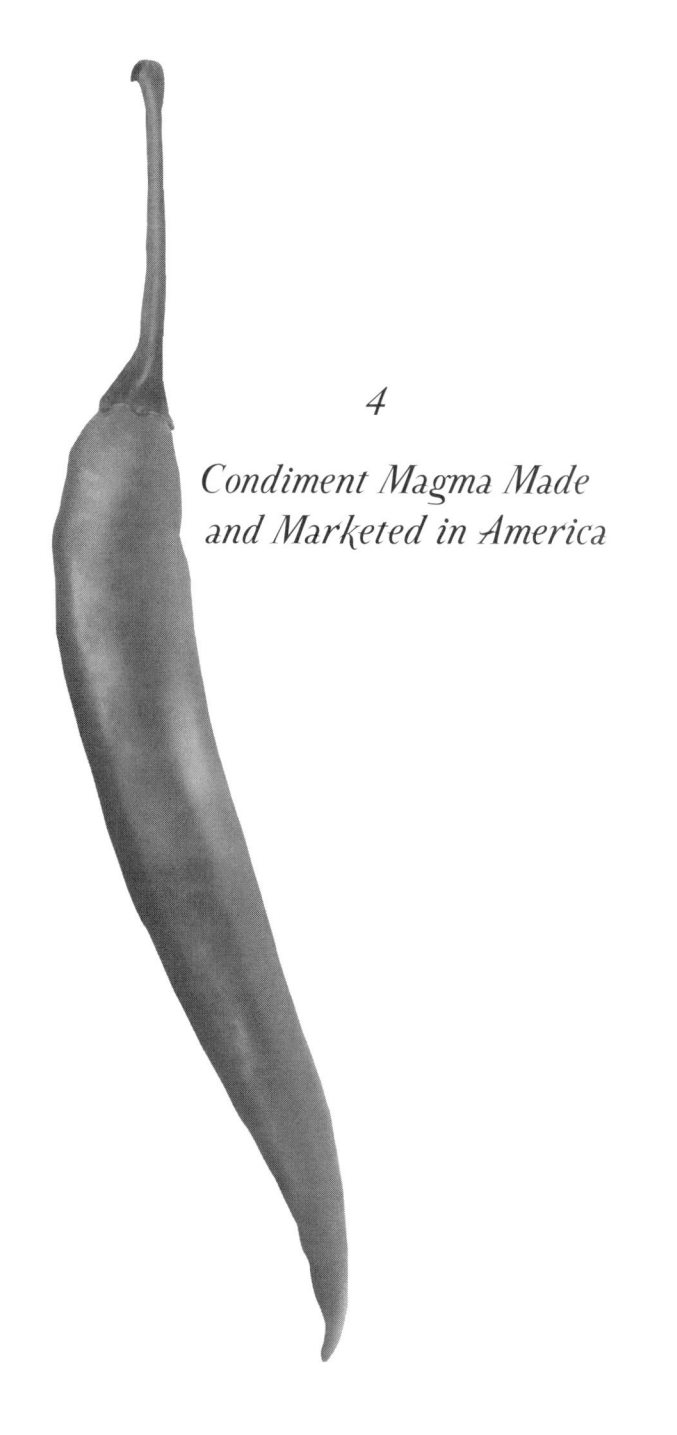

Condiment Magma Made and Marketed in America

> *Gee whiz! Dave, Blair, Jennifer, the other Dave,
> PyroMan, and all the other boys and girls at the
> head of the chile-pepper class have sure done
> all us littler chileheads proud.*
>
> ANONYMOUS SENTIMENTAL CHILEHEAD

Just what is it about the freakin' Americans, anyway? Their love affair with hot sauce rages on and on. No alienation of affection there. No prospect of disaffection. No flameout on the horizon—just more brushfires breaking out all over Painland. And a whole lot of ecstasy and agony in the form of zipless encounters between palates and chile peppers.

Overheated American chileheads always have to be way ahead of the pack. For a long while, Mexico, Jamaica, and Trinidad led the hot-sauce stampede. These countries built reputations as the world's premier hot-sauce producers over a long period of time. Traditional Mexican cuisine is steeped in hot sauce. But as soon as Americans developed a lust for the heat, they started to thrust ahead. America must now be moved to the head of the chile-pepper class. In fact, one could argue that America is the hotbed of worldwide hot-sauce production. It has certainly achieved hegemony in the eyes of chileheads throughout Painland, a metacountry that shares several common borders with the good ol' U.S. of A.

Now, it is true that only certain regions of the U.S. actually produce the sauce in large quantities—the Southwest, southern Louisiana, and, more recently, Texas—but the entire country is a hot hot-sauce consuming zone. In the U.S. there exists an ingenuity and intensity in the preparation and presentation of hot sauces the likes of which the world has never seen. The majority of the world's hot sauce fanatics, and the lunatic fringe of the hot-sauce cult, hail from the land of the free and the home of the brave.

A few years ago, the extraordinary hot-sauce collection of sauce maven Chuck Evans was listed and annotated in *The Hot Sauce Bible*, an essential text penned by Evans himself along with sauce savant Dave DeWitt. As it turned out, most of the items in the Evans collection were manufactured in the United States: 1,194 (or 76 percent of the collection) were homegrown. This just goes to show that in the U.S., hot-sauce production is not controlled by the big commercial manufacturers; it's a cottage industry that has gotten way out of hand.

For at least 200 years, Americans in various parts of the country have savored homemade hot sauce. Over the past 10 years, record numbers of American chileheads have been busy experimenting with new formulas, striving to achieve the perfect incendiary results. In the process, thousands of people have automatically become citizens of Painland. Passports and visas have been issued and temperatures taken. Honorary entitlements have been offered. Now countless Americans hold dual citizenship with Painland. The phenomenon just keeps growing. Hundreds upon hundreds of new brands are introduced in the U.S. every year.

So what sparked this phenomenon, and how did it develop? To encourage an appreciation among novice chileheads for their own history, let's trace America's hot-sauce timeline. Using several sources (most predominantly, the aforementioned *Hot Sauce Bible*, an important resource for chileheads everywhere), I've compiled an abridged list of significant events and developments. Here goes.

- In 1807, the first bottled cayenne sauce surfaces in Massachusetts.
- Between 1840 and 1860, a bird pepper sauce is produced by J. McCollick and Company of New York City.
- In 1849, the first recorded crop of tabasco chiles is grown by a prominent Louisiana banker and legislator, Colonel Maunsell White, on his Deer Range Plantation.
- In 1859, Colonel White manufactures one of the first hot sauces from tabascos. He gives some of these chiles to Edmund McIlhenny, who plants the seeds at his plantation on Avery Island at the southern tip of Louisiana.
- In 1865, the McIlhenny family returns home following the Civil War to find their plantation laid waste; but a few scraggly chile plants survive. McIlhenny uses their seeds to sow a new crop, and over time he rebuilds his plantation and develops his sauce recipe.

- In 1868, McIlhenny fills hundreds of empty cologne bottles with his sauce and sends out samples. The venture is astonishingly successful, and the orders pour in.
- In 1870, McIlhenny patents his Tabasco Hot Pepper Sauce.
- By 1872, McIlhenny has opened an office in London to service the European trade.
- In 1875, Eugene R. Durkee of Brooklyn, New York, applies for a patent on a hexagonal chile-sauce bottle. He goes on to build a large condiment company, and the Durkee brand name exists to this day.
- In 1877, Willam H. Railton, owner of the Chicago Preserving Works, starts producing sauces "prepared from a Mexican formula."
- In 1883, Railton applies for a trademark, and by the next year he's advertising his Chili Colorow Sauce.
- Throughout the 1880s and 1890s, a number of hot sauces come onto the market, including C&D Peppersauce, manufactured by Chace and Duncan of New York City.
- In 1893, Popie Devillier invents Hotter 'n Hell hot sauce. The recipe is handed down through his family for more than 90 years. Then, in 1992, Popie's Hotter 'n Hell Sauce is made available to the public.
- In 1896, rancher Emilio Ortega moves from New Mexico to California, bringing with him some pepper seeds. He establishes a pepper-canning industry in Santa Ana.
- In 1898, former McIlhenny employee B.F. Trappey harvests tabasco chiles from Avery Island seeds and

sells his own sauce under the name B.F. Trappey and Sons. His decision to call his product Tabasco Sauce as well sparks the legendary hot-sauce war with the McIlhenny clan.

- In 1900, the Bergman and Company Pioneer Pickle Factory in Sacramento, California, begins marketing Bergman's Diablo Pepper Sauce; Koonyik Chile Sauce is introduced; Horton-Cato starts manufacturing Royal Pepper Sauce; and Heinz launches its Tabasco Pepper Sauce.
- In 1906, Trappey secures the Tabasco trademark.
- In 1911, the Joseph Campbell Company begins marketing Campbell's Tabasco Ketchup.
- In 1916, Charles E. Erath of New Orleans introduces Extract of Louisiana Pepper, Red Hot Creole Peppersauce.
- In 1917, La Victoria Foods of Los Angeles introduces its Salsa Brava.
- In 1923, Louisiana's Baumer Foods begins manufacturing Crystal Hot Sauce.
- In 1928, Bruce Foods starts to produce Original Louisiana Hot Sauce.
- In 1929, Trappey expands operations to two plants, one in Lafayette and one in New Iberia. The McIlhenny family wins a trademark-infringement suit against Trappey; as a consequence, only McIlhenny sauce can be labeled "Tabasco." Decades of dueling brand names come to an end.
- In 1941, Henry Tanklage establishes a company to market the La Victoria salsa line.

- In 1946, Tanklage assumes the mantle of the entire La Victoria operation, which today manufactures approximately 10 varieties of sauce, including Green Chili Salsa and Red Salsa Jalapeña.
- In 1947, salsa production gets under way in Texas when David and Margaret Pace open a small food-packing operation San Antonio; their picante sauce will prove to be immensely popular.
- In 1952, Tanklage's La Victoria Foods unveils America's first commercial taco sauce.
- In 1955, La Preferida starts producing a line of salsas.
- In 1975, Patti Swidler of Tucson, Arizona, launches Desert Rose Salsa, a line specifically designed to be sold in specialty food shops.
- In 1979, Dan Jardine of Austin, Texas, creates a line of commercial salsas.
- In 1980, the El Paso Chile Company, also based in Texas, is founded by Norma and W. Park Kerr.
- Throughout the 1980s, the hot-sauce craze builds in the United States.
- In 1981, Chris Way opens a seafood restaurant called Barnacle Bill's in St. Augustine, Florida, where he serves a hot sauce containing datil peppers. His Dat'l Do It sauce becomes a local legend, and one of Way's regular customers, a VP of the Wynn-Dixie supermarket chain, offers to carry it at his outlets. There are currently a number of Dat'l Do It products on the market, including Hellish Relish, a favorite of Mr. Chilehead.

- In 1983, the Panola Pepper Company of Lake Providence, Louisiana, starts selling a hot sauce made by one Bubber Brown from his mom's recipe. Also, Durkee-French introduces Frank's Red Hot Cayenne Pepper Sauce with an advertising blitz; Red Hot goes on to challenge Tabasco for U.S. market share.
- In 1986, Miguel's Stowe Away of Vermont launches a salsa line. Sauces & Salsas Limited of Columbus, Ohio, brings Montezuma hot-pepper sauces and salsas to the marketplace.
- In 1987, America's largest salsa manufacturer, Pace Foods of San Antonio, sues its biggest competitor, Pet Food's Old El Paso. Pace claims that Pet has stolen its label, its bottle shape, and its slogan. Pace also finds itself threatened by another major competitor, Geo. A. Hormel. Hormel licenses the brand name Chi-Chi's and subsequently captures a large share of the market. Dave DeWitt (aka the Pope of Peppers), Robert Spiegel, and Nancy Gerlach found *Chile Pepper* magazine. It's still the principal national publication championing all things hot.
- In 1988, Pace and Pet settle out of court after Pet agrees to change the bottle and label of Old El Paso. Boston's Lisa Lammé opens Le Saucier, perhaps the first retail shop to specialize in hot sauces. Macayo Foods of Phoenix introduces a line of taco sauces in plastic bottles. The first National Fiery Foods Show is held in El Paso, Texas. Though it starts with just 37 exhibitors, the show will eventually feature hundreds of exhibitors and highlight thousands of hot sauces.

- Between 1985 and 1990, sales of Mexican sauces increase a whopping 79 percent.
- Between 1988 and 1992, the percentage of American families buying salsa rises from 16 to 36 percent.
- In 1989, the first chipotle sauces are made by U.S. manufacturers. Chris Schlesinger of the East Coast Grill in Cambridge, Massachusetts, sends his Inner Beauty hot sauce out into the world. By this time, some 35 Louisiana sauce manufacturers are producing about 100 different brands of hot sauce.
- In 1990, the citizens of Los Angeles consume 3.3 million gallons of hot sauce, making the City of Angels honorary capital of Painland. Pace Foods delivers several thousand bottles of Pace Picante Sauce to U.S. troops stationed in the Saudi Arabian desert. Austin beats San Antonio in the first *Austin Chronicle* Hot Sauce Contest. Several competitors subsequently bottle and market their winning entries.
- In 1992, salsa replaces ketchup as America's number-one condiment. Dr. Paul W. Bosland founds the Chile Pepper Institute.
- In 1994, with over 350 entries, the *Austin Chronicle* Hot Sauce Contest becomes the world's largest.
- Throughout the 1990s, Dave Hirschkopf's career as a savvy saucemeister takes off and soars, thanks to his murderous Insanity sauce. He founds Dave's Gourmet and spins other products into the line. Hirschkopf kicks off the extract craze, and his introduction of insanely hot products into the marketplace becomes a catalyst for everything that follows in Painland. Blair

Gardner inaugurates and shepherds his Death Sauce line, so called because, in the words of its creator, the sauces "take you to the brink of heat intoxication and drop you off just short of eternity for a 'Feel Alive!' sensation."

- In 1995, *The Great Hot Sauce Book* is published. Its author, Jennifer Trainer Thompson—the "Queen of Hot," according to Associated Press—is the creator of Jump Up and Kiss Me hot sauces.
- In 1997, the inaugural Scovie Awards for best hot sauces are held; a Scovie becomes the most prestigious honor a sauce maker can receive.
- In 1998, the International Society of Hot Sauce Aficionados is founded. The goal of the organization's membership is to sample all existing hot sauces. In the words of its founders, "Recognizing that only the select few with vision, fortitude and dedication will attempt to accomplish this worthy goal, the ISHSA was founded to provide information, encouragement, community and access to the more difficult to procure hot sauces of the planet."
- From the early 1990s to the present, the Internet becomes a vital resource for retailers of hot sauce and all chile-related products. The Ring of Fire, with over 400 member sites, establishes itself as the nexus of saucedom on the Net, and on the planet.

So ends our timeline. And where do we stand today? The way of the present and the future for chileheads is, of course, the Internet. The Net continues to foster solidarity among chileheads. In cyberspace, a chilehead can exchange information and lore with like-minded individuals as well as shop online for the most exotic and difficult-to-obtain hot sauces or pepper-related products.

Three years into the new millennium, the hot-sauce wave breaking over America shows no signs of ebbing. The red-hot chile pepper still reigns supreme! Indubitably, this will be the millennium of the chile pepper. We'll probably see it being exported to the moon or Mars within the next hundred years. Chile peppers off-planet? The odyssey continues.

5

*Dave's Insanity:
An Evangelical Hot-Sauce
Maker's Jihad*

> *Every night when I go to bed, I thank the Lord my boys are fed, yes I thank Our Father in Heaven for our daily bread, but I always sneak in a line thanking Dave for his Insanity Hot Sauce and what it does to the inside of my head. Hallowed be his name, too.*
>
> ANONYMOUS CHILEHEAD, OVERHEARD IN CONFESSIONAL

Every madness has elements of the divine or the demonic. And some even have a method. The madness of Dave Hirschkopf, the straitjacketed genius behind some of the hottest sauces on the planet, has it all. Hirschkopf has created some divine concoctions that are demonically hot. Angels may inspire him in his work, but there are demons driving him to the extremes of heat. As we shall see, there is also a whole lot of method in the way he's married heaven and hell.

Dave is the proprietor of a California concern called Dave's Gourmet Specialty Food Company. He markets over 60 products, most of them satanically hot. His list of condiments range from habañero-infused peanuts, olives, green beans, and dill pickles to the now-legendary Special Reserve Hot Sauce, a sauce that is truthfully advertised as being one of the hottest in the world.

Hirschkopf's customer base gives whole new meaning to the term "cult following." Dave is nothing less than an evangelist for fiery foods, and we, his customers, are all born-agains; we're a parched flock that laps up each new product Dave sees fit to unleash upon us. Good Christian soldiers ain't got nothing on us chileheads. We chileheads love Dave, truly, madly, deeply. But why, exactly? Because Dave loves us in turn. Aren't his widely available elixirs of life, satanic ambrosias, bottled magmas proof enough of that love?

Perhaps we also love Dave because his products give us a unique opportunity for vicarious enjoyment. What true chilehead does not secretly (or perhaps openly) revel in the sight of novice chile tasters falling to their knees, red-faced, hyperventilating, as though in the grip of a seizure? Sweating profusely, arms outstretched martyr-style, a stricken expression distorting their features, they broadcast a mute appeal for mercy. Then they'll attempt to save themselves through a series of amusing antics: gargling gallons of cold ale, plunging their heads into cold water to extinguish the fire that rages in their heads . . .

Dave's Insanity has the power to reduce the unwary taster to this sorry condition because it's a hot sauce as lethal as they come. In its mildest form, it's at least 10 times as strong as the ubiquitous Tabasco, and at its most volcanic, it rivals Montezuma. Dave likes to brag about this. He's been quoted many times as saying that he's personally responsible for hospitalizing more people with his Insanity than any other hot-sauce maker has with his/her own. And since he wears a straitjacket and a satisfied smirk while making this claim, does it make us love him all the more? Is his madness just a more robust version of our own, as survivors of the heat? Are we all candidates for the asylum? Should our families commit us? Hard to say.

Dave once said of his Special Reserve: "It just ain't going to get any hotter than this." Well, that may no longer be true, but it was when he said it. Dave's Gourmet labels exemplify truth in advertising, of necessity. The sauces are potentially so hazardous to the health and sanity of its users that the bottles carry explicit warnings: contents must be kept away from exposed skin, the eyes, children, pets; people with heart or respiratory conditions should steer clear of the stuff.

Comedian Buddy Hackett once paid a singular tribute to Dave's culinary invention by saying, "I'm 71 years old, and because of Insanity Sauce, I will live to be 100 . . . and my ass will catch up later" (quoted on the Dave's Gourmet Web site, www.davesgourmet.com). To taste Dave's hot sauce is to engage in an act of gustatory pyromania; it is to invite intestinal perdition. As the habañero extract burns your lips and tongue and anus, as it sparks that awesome endorphin rush in your brain, you realize that you've put yourself in the hands of the devil himself. And, for Christ's sake, don't reach for a glass of water—it will only spread the pain across several agonizing orders of internal magnitude. Because the sauces are oil-based, water spreads the heat, turning a bad situation into a crisis. Of course, "bad" is an ambiguous term. We chileheads want the pain, we savor it. The potent blend of flavor and extreme heat is a rare and exotic blessing. The taste of pain is transcendental.

At hot-sauce festivals throughout the U.S., Dave, temporarily relieved of his straitjacket, hands out toothpicks dipped in the sauce to courageous tasters. A mere toothpick's worth will buy you a taste of pure hell— trauma, followed by taste-bud nirvana. Perhaps the best remedy for the heat is a large glass of cold milk. Sorbet is also good. And vanilla ice cream can be quite effective —but lay off the ice water.

The Insanity takes a few minutes to hit. During this deceptively mild interlude, your body is prepped for the initial slow burn. You get a handle on the slow burn, and then the fireball hits and you're on the floor. It's no joke. Dave himself insists that his hot sauce should be taken very, very seriously. He advises his customers to use a scant drop to spice a dish—a large pot of chile con carne, for instance. However, Dave is capable of seeing the lighter side to all of this. At a recent hot-sauce festival, he told a story about a woman who had purchased two gallons of his hottest sauce "for her personal use." One can only wonder if her partner in life was the intended victim of the sauce. Had legal papers been served? Was the lady planning an excruciating torture regimen? Or did she simply love the afterburn?

Dave's reputation as hot-sauce subculture guru was initially based on the fact that he was the first sauce maker to use capsaicin in concentrated form. Capsaicin is the substance that gives chile peppers their heat and their bite. Now Dave is the leader of the global extract craze. These days, Dave's Gourmet operates out of a sizeable warehouse-and-office setup. The company has 13 employees, and demand for its products is on the rise. You might say Dave is poised to seize control of Painland (but perhaps he is already its implicit monarch).

Did Dave embark on the road to chilehead supremacy the day he opened a little burrito joint in College Park, Maryland, called Burrito Madness? Or did it all begin when he stumbled upon habañero peppers for the first time while employed as Mexico City station chief by the Central Intelligence Agency? Did he prepare himself for that unorthodox career by earning a degree in Soviet studies from Boston University? Dave stories are legion, and no one really knows what got the ball rolling, but Dave himself tells us that the drunkards of College Park likely gave that ball a good nudge. Reminiscing about his Burrito Madness days, he said:

> Being in a college town, we used to get our share of inebriated folks visiting our establishment and, at times, they could get pretty rowdy. Basically, I have a sick mind. We were open till late, and drunks would come in and be really obnoxious. I thought, "How can I get rid of them?" I started thinking about what makes chiles hot, and I came up with this really hot sauce that I would put in their order . . . I figured that if our sauce was really hot, these people would be too distracted to steal or break anything. My plan was to mix up the hottest sauce I could and put it on the burritos. The plan worked at first. Then people began asking for the sauce, which was served in a paper cup. Some of my customers claimed that you

had to be insane to use the stuff. I was shocked when people ran out the doors sweating only to come back the next day to buy some sauce for themselves and their friends. It was amusing. So I decided to make the hottest sauce in the world. Once I found out plenty of people were making sauces out of the hottest peppers, I figured I'd make a sauce out of pepper extracts. That's how Insanity Sauce was invented.

In inventing that sauce, Dave had performed a public service. One wonders how many of his inebriated customers poured a little on a burrito, joined AA, got on the wagon, and gave themselves over to Dave's Insanity. How many successfully evicted their inner wussy? We will never know. But these people don't have to worry about their livers anymore. Their larynxes? That's another matter. My vocal chords have been scorched more than once by Dave's brews. But it's better to lose your voice than your life. Agreed?

Dave's Insanity has gone down in history as one of the first extreme-heat sauces, and it's certainly the most notorious. It made such a splash that Dave decided to become a sauce entrepreneur. He entered the 1993 National Fiery Foods Show, and his entry was promptly banned from the show. The holy father of Pepperdom, Dave DeWitt, producer of the (renamed) National Fiery Foods and Barbecue Show, has explained: "Insanity Sauce was just too hot for the normal method of tasting—getting a dollop on a cracker or tortilla. So we eventually had to come up with a method to allow the tasting of superhot sauces, and there are now many of them to be sampled. There are no problems today." Show officials decided that the only proper tasting method for the hottest sauces was taking a dab on the end of a toothpick. Given the intensity of many sauces these days, it seems a wise solution.

As it turned out, the ban had some real benefits. It lent an aura of danger to Dave's product that fed right into an effective advertising campaign. Since 1993, Dave has won numerous awards, including several Scovies. Recently, he was presented with a Scovie in the gift basket/box category for his Chile Head Survival Kit and another, in the snacks category, for his Insanity Popcorn. He has also garnered honors from the National Association for the Specialty Food Trade, the International Mustard Festival, the Fiery Food Challenge, *Food Distribution Magazine*, and the Atlanta Gourmet Show, among many others.

When Dave's Insanity sauce first caught fire, its creator relocated from San Bruno, California, to San Francisco. He worked as a mortgage broker for a while—can you even imagine Dave as a mortgage broker?—and sold his sauce on the side. Soon, however, he quit his day job and dove headfirst and full time into the sauce. Over the past decade, he has launched over 100 products. Says Dave, "I am basically a chef, and I love to make a new recipe. We have experimented with just about everything, and some of our products have really made for great sales."

Arguably, Dave's unorthodox experimentation with, and marketing of, hot consumables led to the glorious birth of the truly hot habañero sauce subculture in America. When habañero sauces first trickled into the mainstream, they were few and far between. Now, of course, the trickle has become a flood. Dave led the way, and in the process he provoked more controversy and aroused more public interest than any other hot-sauce maker. He's been the subject of feature articles in magazines as diverse as *Men's Health* and *Playboy*; he's appeared on *Good Morning America*, *Today*, and *Sunday Morning* with Charles Kuralt; newspaper reports published nationwide have covered his exploits. Dave has become a legend to chileheads and the public at large.

Products like Dave's Special Reserve—which boasts 750,000 Scoville units—added a good deal of luster to the legend, but I'd be doing Hirschkopf an injustice if I failed to mention his other offerings here. The best-known Dave's line is Insanity, a line that includes some insanely hot sauces, but Dave purveys some milder concoctions as well. Products bearing the Dave's Gourmet seal range from hot sauces to salsas to Mad Mushroom and Udderly Insane cheese. Dave also produces the Jump Up and Kiss Me line with spicy food auteur Jennifer Trainer Thompson; that line includes hot Caribbean sauces, a chipotle sauce, and a chipotle salsa. Sharing space beneath the Dave's Gourmet umbrella are the products of the Joe's Sauces brand: Soak Sauce, with garlic and bourbon; Grilled Fruit and Fish Glaze; and

Roasted Garlic Grill Sauce. Rounding out the Dave's catalog are Bloody Mary and margarita mixes, barbecue sauces, pickled green beans, mustards, salsas, and a full array of seasonings, candies, and snacks. Needless to say, everything Hirschkopf puts his name on has flair and sting.

But there's more to life than flair and sting. Dave's products, particularly his Insanity Sauce, have been shown to have certain practical applications in daily life. Some people have used it to deter animals from wreaking havoc in the garden. Others swear that the stuff is a potent aphrodisiac. And the Marines employ it during initiation rites for new recruits. (Hazed with hot sauce? You don't even want to think about it.)

Let's get back to the flair and sting. I can personally attest to the fact that a few drops of Dave's Special Reserve Millennium Hot Sauce will infuse your standard spaghetti sauce with sublime and sulfuric flavor—and an order of torment found only at certain levels of Dantean hell. And it's all because of the extract, the oleoresin capsicum.

As I've said, Dave is solely responsible for the extract craze. Once he'd distilled the extract, he could focus on what he loves most: donning the big white hat and screwing around in the kitchen. "Working from a chef's perspective," says Dave, "we have been able to experiment and design foods that are not only fiery hot, but very tasty . . . In developing products, we have a creative process that has to take in several factors: Will the new product live up to the Insanity name? Will it sell? Hot sauces actually don't turn too fast, so you need other products like a great pasta sauce. We experimented with all kinds of tomatoes and found that the heirloom variety was the tastiest, and we developed two best-selling sauces, Red Heirloom and Yellow Heirloom."

These days, Dave no longer makes his own products, which indicates just how big he's grown. He's contracted with several large food manufacturers to do the job for him according to the exacting standards he has set, and he keeps close watch over them to ensure quality control. With this increased production capacity has come increased sales potential, and Dave's Gourmet has seen excellent sales throughout California and in New York, Pennsylvania, Illinois, Florida, and Texas. The products are also sold in Canada, England, and several European countries. The wildly popular Dave's Gourmet Web site moves a lot of product as well.

Dave's favorite book is *The Old Man and the Sea*, by Ernest Hemingway. Why? Perhaps because the old man's long and harrowing battle to control the mighty marlin, bend it to his will, and reel it in mirrors Dave's own struggle to control the powerful capsaicin. Not to mention the struggle of Dave's faithful customers, who do battle internally with his nearly lethal hot sauces. Those of us who triumph over the heat may perhaps experience a thrill similar to that which transports Hemingway's old man.

With his hot sauces, Dave challenges us to incinerate our palates with a fruit that surely comes from Avernus, or an even deeper and hotter hell. Did the serpent introduce that fruit into Eden? Was it a habañero, not an apple, that Eve offered Adam? Probably. Yes, Dave's concoctions challenge us to overcome our weaknesses and to embrace an order of heat that only Dante himself would have understood. They challenge our ability to withstand an inferno that, once raging within us, is consummately difficult to extinguish.

Dave takes his inferno in a bottle and the challenge it embodies to hot-sauce festivals across the U.S.A. The vision of Dave wearing his trademark straitjacket is one that we chileheads anticipate with great pleasure. Despite the uniform, Dave is more like a priest than a madman. He seems to be saying, "Share my insanity!" or, "My sins are yours, and I alone exonerate you! Let my Insanity sauce deliver you from evil, for I am the Resurrection and the Life!"

Dave, our beloved Dave, your jihad is only in its infancy. May it continue for at least 10,000 years! You understand only too well that the pepper extract—like the true protagonist of Frank Herbert's Dune books: the spice mélange—can transform the universe and lead us all out of darkness.

6

Fragments of Agony and Ecstasy: Some Painful and Pleasurable Moments Painfully and Pleasurably Remembered

It doesn't matter who you are, or what you've done, or think you can do. There's a confrontation with destiny awaiting you. Somewhere, there is a chile you cannot eat.

DANIEL PINKWATER

What bound me to the chile peppers? They alone reminded me that I am still a human being.

ANONYMOUS CHILEHEAD

As I mentioned in my introduction, the spice experiences of my youth were formative. They sowed their seeds in my forebrain and my appetite and my palate, internal fields that lay fallow until I was older. Those seeds then sprouted into an addiction and, subsequently, an obsession. They affirmed for me my first, best destiny: chilehead.

The heavenly aromas of turmeric, curry powder, cumin, and other spices in my parent's pantry did more than tickle my sinus cavities—they enlivened my palate and placed their coruscating aureole upon my imagination. In my mind, I traveled up and down the old spice routes, and as I explored I realized that there was something erotic about the spice as well. Indeed, a kind of erotic melancholy penetrated the atmosphere of the pantry, alleviated periodically by visits from Vicky, the little blonde-haired girl from next door. That temptress and chilehead-in-waiting was seemingly induced by the scent of the spice to shed her clothes and any inhibitions she might have had where yours truly was concerned . . . Well, we were just children.

Of course, at the tender age of my initiation (into Painland, I mean), I did not think there was anything extraordinary about the spice—it was just there. But then I began to notice that when family friends came over for dinner, controversies over the heat level of the food would often erupt, and I did find that odd. It didn't seem to happen in other people's homes. Some of our guests would turn red in the face, some even became apoplectic. Too hot? Really? Hmmm . . . I was perplexed. "Is this person a wuss, or what?" I would say to myself. But guess what? Our red-faced dinner guests would inevitably return to our table for more of the same.

Other chile writers have eloquently described their own Proustian madeleine experiences. For them, of course, the madeleine that triggers the flood of memory is the pepper, with its pungent bite and aroma. The chile pepper retains the power to transport them to the Painland of their youth, the place where they learned just how marvelous and electrifying the taste of pain can be. Once you cross the border into that land, there is no turning back.

And why would one ever want to? Turn back, I mean. Once the pepper latches onto your palate, you're in the hands of a higher power—I mean fate. The chile ministers to both body and soul. Addiction is an affliction of both. But this addiction is restorative. There is no attrition. There is also no possibility of remission—once you're diagnosed, that's all folks. End of story. It's all about submission. Willing submission. The old saw "No pain, no gain" still holds sway in Painland. And what do we all have to look forward to? Further confrontations with destiny: somewhere, somehow, there really is a pepper that we cannot eat.

I again acknowledge that none of this is new. Red-hot chile peppers have always played a prominent role in the native cuisines of the Americas. In the fifteenth century, Bartolomé de las Casas, one of the first Spaniards to write about Mexico, offered this astute observation of Native Americans: "Without chile, they don't think they are eating!" Well, the ranks of chileheads who side with the Natives in this regard (myself included) are still swelling, centuries later. We all carry chilehead emergency kits containing small bottles of sauce, little plastic bags filled with chile powder, and shakers of habañero flakes. It is essential that we be ready at all times to treat the bland food that we are presented with over and over again in the course of our daily lives. We've learned that the food of the cattle is never spicy enough for our needs. It screams out for chile intervention.

When you are truly into the hot pepper, you become aware of a certain sensation rising above the immediate visceral pain that accompanies its ingestion. Amorphous, nebulous—a higher order of drug. There is a wanting that becomes a needing that becomes a yearning. You are separated from the cattle—the uninitiated—by that need. Much like a vampire, one assumes, who needs to drink nightly. (Bats and fanged beings are often depicted on hot-sauce bottles, by the way. One example is Vampfire Hot Sauce, whose label depicts Count Dracula readying himself for a repast; it also bears the legend, "Made up the road from Transylvania, L.A.")

Any true pepper fan will confess to the pleasurable yearning. At the end of a long day, I look forward to my evening meal—a lovely flank steak, say, cooked medium-rare—but it is the sliced or diced jalapeño peppers I'll have with that steak that fire my imagination. The peppers are a true reward. They turn an otherwise humble repast into a dimensionally rich, sensorially inviting, and strangely exciting adventure. In other words, the pepper is essential to the chilehead's quality of life. As Amal Naj says in his superb book *Peppers: A Story of Hot Pursuits*, "Take the pepper away from the pepper eater and he withdraws and slips into a general malaise at the dinner table. He may even choose to starve. Or he may go to extraordinary lengths to procure his pepper. Notice the note of warmth and excitement when he talks about his favorite pepper. Listen to his 'ah!' when he bites into his choice pod. Notice, too, how amid sweating and gasping he reaches for more and more of the hot stuff and silently rocks between the crests of undulating pain and pleasure" (207).

"Silently rock[ing] between the crests of undulating pain and pleasure." It's eloquently stated. What Naj describes here has a strong resemblance to opiate addiction.

I am certain that those of us who are held tight in the vise of this addiction will never be cured. We must surrender to it at every mealtime with dignity and forbearance. In this chapter, I will describe a few of my own experiences, alternately hilarious and terrifying, as a wanton chile addict.

But first things first. Before we proceed with tales of agony and ecstasy, we must understand a few things about our friends in the brain—I mean the endorphins. The high from an endorphin rush can last from 5 to 15 minutes, and your brain releases endorphins every time you eat hot peppers. What actually transpires is this: When capsaicin interfaces with the nerve endings in your tongue and mouth, the pain messengers in those nerve endings craftily imitate burning sensations, which are then express-couriered to the brain. Of course, capsaicin does not actually burn your mouth the way red-hot embers would. The reason the pain snitches, or neurotransmitters, send this false signal to the brain is still somewhat of a mystery. In any case, in a lightning-fast survival-reflex maneuver, the brain instructs the organism to dump the capsaicin at all costs. Hence, your heart rate increases, your breathing accelerates, your mouth salivates copiously, your gastrointestinal tract hits overdrive, and your head, face, and neck sweat profusely.

Now, here's the rub. As your brain, intent on expelling the capsaicin, which it senses is damaging your body, does what it can to help and produces its natural painkillers, endorphins. The released endorphins create an effect similar to a syringe of morphine plunged into a vein—an ultra-narcotic chile high.

Since the pepper does no real harm to the organism, the effect is all smoke and mirrors. Despite the way it feels as it takes control of your mouth, the pepper will not burn off a layer of epidermis the way scalding water will (I can attest to this, since I love to take baths in almost boiling water)—if it's not extract, that is. So, strangely, a painful bite of habañero is really a tidy dose of painkiller. Bite the habañero again, endure another burst of pain, and your brain will release still more endorphins. Without those blessed endorphins, we would all be deadheads. Their slow release continues like a mental orgasm, the ejaculate invisible. And—Lord, oh Lord—what a pleasure it is!

Those of you who look upon the antics of Mr. Chilehead and other pepper eaters with amusement or disdain should meditate for a moment on this matter of the endorphin release. Why is it that we crave hotter and hotter sauces, some so hot that we must sign legal waivers in order to obtain them? Why is it that we continually subject ourselves to the taste of pain? Because the endorphins tempt us with their promise of more pleasure through pain.

Now that we all understand this, let me present my first fragment of agony and/or ecstasy.

> *Scorpion venom ain't got nothin' on The Source.*
> *But it's a damn good aphrodisiac.*

ANONYMOUS CHILEHEAD, OVERHEARD IN HOSPITAL BED

I was in Tijuana, and Miranda was with me. We were in that happenin' town to relax and avail ourselves of the local pepper cuisine. One evening at twilight—a transcendently lovely mauve twilight punctuated by flitting bats—we stumbled into a sprawling, low-ceilinged bar. Of course, it's not wise to walk around Tijuana after sunset, especially the outer reaches of Revolución Avenue. But anyway, there we were. And we almost stumbled right back out of that bar, for at the back was a large aquarium jammed with nightmarish, hyperactive black shapes. Scorpions. Dozens of 'em. Jet black, shiny as car hoods, tails on high, claws open and grasping, rending, tearing . . .

I wanted to leave forthwith. I don't much like bugs. And in my opinion, a scorpion is just an overgrown and rather nasty-looking bug. However, it looked like I would need a handgun to take out one of those critters. Or a flame-thrower. But Miranda was tired, her feet hurt, and she wanted a drink. Despite my misgivings, I relented, and we sat down. After all, the scorpions appeared to be hermetically sealed in their aquarium (I later discovered that it was actually their holding pen). Well, I thought we were safe. I was wrong. But how could I have known?

I told Miranda to put her tired feet up on my knee, and I started to massage them. Her toes immediately perked up; her arches arched—always a good sign. The bar's atmosphere was informal, and there were few other customers. A couple near the door was laughing together, and there was some lively banter farther down the bar—locals, not tourists. I ordered a rum and Coke and Miranda requested her usual Bloody Mary. "Does your lady like it hot?" the bartender asked. "Yes, very," I replied. We sat back and prepared to unwind.

"Gee whiz, what did they put in this?" said Miranda, holding her glass up to the light. "There's liquid fire in my glass." She was starting to enjoy herself. It was then that I noticed row upon row of hot-sauce bottles behind the bar. There must have been more than 500 of them. Instantly, Painland beckoned.

I approached the bartender, a bear of a man sporting a black handlebar mustache. "That's quite a collection of hot sauces you have there," I ventured, squinting at the bottles. There were many brands I had never seen before. I started to salivate. My palms started to sweat. Like most bartenders in most dives in most parts of the world, this fellow was quite genial, despite his forbidding bulk.

"Are they for sale?" I inquired in an instinctive bid to expand my collection and punish my palate. He replied, "I am afraid most are not for sale. Property of the house." Disappointment washed over me. "But you can buy a bottle of the house sauce, if you like. It's called Scorpion Sting. We make it ourselves. It's one mean motherfucker of a sauce. Superhot. Would you and your lady friend like to try a little?"

"Why not?" I replied "Thanks kindly." I immediately took to the label, which bore a crude image of a black scorpion rearing up on its hind legs. There was no text —on the back there was just a skull and crossbones that looked like it had been stamped on by hand. The bottle was flat and flask-shaped. I decided to buy a case of the sauce even before we'd sampled it. "How would you like it? By the toothpick or by the spoon?" inquired the bartender, who had introduced himself as Miguel. I asked him how hot the sauce was. Miguel admitted that it was "very, very hot," but he added, "What is hot to you might be lukewarm to another." I was really starting to like this fellow.

Miguel uncorked the bottle. When I dine in a restaurant, I always ask my date to sniff the cork and taste the wine first. Such is my archaic notion of chivalry. But as far as hot sauce is concerned, I do the initial testing myself, and I make no exceptions to this rule. I asked Miguel for a spoon, shunning the toothpick, and with it I took the plunge. It was a true taste experience. A lot of sauce has passed under this bridge, and much of it has begun to taste the same. But Scorpion Sting was different. It had a unique persona—a very perky one. When it hit my tongue, it was not immediately apparent to me that this stuff would open the door to hell. By the time I'd ingested my third teaspoon, my tongue was swollen and sweating blood. Miranda, who by then had taken a hit herself, seemed to be having trouble breathing. Her cheeks were brick red, and she was sweating profusely. But she looked damn fine. Damn fine, really. As for myself, I was starting to feel the true interiority of the heat, and, truth to tell, I was a little randy.

Miranda was flushed, and her nipples seemed preternaturally erect under her tight-fitting purple shirt. Sweat dappled her forehead like dew. I was aroused. I downed a fourth teaspoon, and that was the real kicker. My swollen tongue was impeding my speech, and I was having trouble making myself understood. Indeed, I must have sounded retarded. As I struggled to tell Miranda how beautiful she looked, my words grew unwieldy. And other things were growing, too. The fire raging in my anesthetized mouth was also raging below my waist. I urgently wanted to put that lower fire out, but we were in a public place.

For centuries, chiles have enjoyed a reputation for being an aphrodisiac, and when I was still quite young, I discovered that this reputation was well earned. But in Tijuana I had my peak experience. Do chiles ignite the flames of passion? Yes, absolutely. They turn your whole being into one big firecracker. Even the Aztecs used them as an aphrodisiac, mixing them with other aphrodisiac plants, such as cocoa and vanilla.

In that scorpion bar, my vision blurred a little, but I attributed that to sweat in my eyes, not a cerebral hemorrhage. That blurring, however—along with a sense of spatial dislocation and a raging erection—constituted one very funky chile high. I felt a weird frisson, and then I was overtaken by a hyperclarity. My thoughts turned to the sauce, and I pondered its ingredients. A truly exotic chile with sexual healing properties? I caught

Miguel's eye and gestured helplessly at the depleted sauce bottle. Then I pointed, with reluctance, to the scorpion tank. He gave me a knowing smile and nodded sagely. There was nothing more to say.

In an effort to protect both the innocent and the perverted, I'll end this anecdote right here. But I will say that Miranda and I could not get ourselves back to the hotel fast enough, and the damn taxi-driver cast a voyeurish eye over the proceedings in the back seat. Later, I read a newspaper report about a baby boom in Tijuana, and I couldn't help wondering whether Scorpion Sting had anything to do with it. Is scorpion venom an aphrodisiac? I don't know. I do know that chiles are. Perhaps a blend of the two would give Viagra a run for its money.

I eventually ran out of the Sting, and on a subsequent visit to Tijuana I tried to replenish my supply, but I found that the bar had been razed and a liquor store erected in its place. Over the years, I've tried other Scorpion hot sauces, such as Scorpion Xtreme, whose label reads, "Don't get bit by this Scorpion, because it might be your last bite." It's a great hot sauce, but, sadly, it's venom-free. The same goes for Scorpio's Curse Scorpion Venom and all the rest. Maybe Scorpion Sting is best left to become an urban legend.

These days, we chileheads are spoiled by the ubiquity of hot sauce. In the U.S., there are specialty stores aplenty where heat fiends load their shopping carts with the sauce, throwing in fresh and dried chiles for good measure, not to mention habañero- and jalapeño-based salsas, spice mixtures, pastes, extracts, chutneys, vinegars, and oils. Condiments we could only have dreamed about a few years ago now abound. Then there's the snack food: chile candies, chile chips, chile popcorn—the list is endless. So is the list of chile-related merchandise: T-shirts, baseball caps, aprons, boxer shorts printed with rampant chile peppers—all manner of chile tchotchkes. Chile festivals are proliferating and chileheads are running amok everywhere.

As I've said elsewhere, the U.S. takes the cake in this regard. My native Canada has been slower to embrace fiery foods. While things are now heating up significantly north of the Canada-U.S. border, the culinary climate has historically been lukewarm. But back in the bland old days, there were always a few exceptions—as the following fragment illustrates.

In the late 1980s, I went to Toronto to meet an artist on whose work I was writing a monograph for the Art Gallery of Ontario. The city's famous Queen Street West district was much different back then—same hustle and bustle, but the chain stores hadn't moved in yet, and there was a lot of funky merchandise to tempt the intrepid shopper. Walking up Queen one evening, I came upon a little store selling Caribbean imports. The door opened as I passed, and a scent wafted out onto the street. I stood transfixed. It was the scent of my parents' pantry.

A warm cascade of spice-related memories washed over me. I stepped over the threshold into a spicy Garden of Eden, and my heart started racing. The store's shelves were packed with hot-sauce bottles, all imports, most of which I'd never seen before. "Can I help you, chief?" asked the cheerful proprietor. "Yes, but I'm speechless," I said, gesticulating wildly at the groaning shelves. "So much sauce!"

The sheer wealth of sauce overwhelmed me. The sight of so many hot sauces in such close proximity filled me with a joy that verged on the carnal. I was titillated. There were lovely Matouks, there were bottles of Aunt May's Red Pepper Sauce, and there were scores of more obscure offerings, the likes of which I had never seen before (and haven't encountered since). "How? Why?" I muttered helplessly. "I cum from Jamaica, mon, and I jast luv da sauce, mon. It push all ma buttons, mon." Well, I knew exactly what he meant. "My mum keeps sending dem, mon, and my auntie." It sounded like the supply-route was secure.

"I must have them," I thought. "I simply must have them." Back then, there wasn't an establishment in Montreal that could match the hot-sauce selection that glistened here before my eyes—I was certain of it. So, 93 sauces and a lot of cash exchanged hands on Queen Street West that night. I had the bottles shipped to my home in Montreal, and when they arrived I luxuriated in their exotic, unfamiliar labels and the gorgeous colors of their contents. I was a happy man, because I'd renewed my passport to Painland.

After that, whenever I planned a trip to Toronto, I added a visit to that import shop to my agenda, which already included regular stops at places like Shopsys, for salamis, and Correnti, for cigars. I'd made several treks to the place before that tragic autumn evening when I discovered that it was all over. Arriving at the store, I felt my heart sink. I tasted ashes. Where I'd once inhaled the heavenly scent of spice and surveyed shelves of colorful bottles, I now beheld racks of trendy clothing. I never did learn what happened to the shop and its savvy spicemeister. Years later, I am still haunted by a visceral sense of loss, for those Jamaican sauces educated my palate and whetted my appetite for more.

Since that first serendipitous evening on Queen Street, I've made much larger hot-sauce purchases—including some very satisfactory ones on eBay and other Internet sites—but that purchase was by far the most memorable. The recollection warms my soul on frigid winter nights.

Each year, chileheads gather at festivals across the land to commune with one another and celebrate their shared passion. Those of us who were fortunate enough (and we were several thousandfold) to attend the first annual Houston Hot Sauce Festival remember that the event was marked by a wonderful feeling of (chilehead) community and an atmosphere of exuberance. Inaugurated in 1999, the festival was the brilliant conception of event promoter Carol Steffan. It's mounted every September, and the proceeds benefit the Stehlin Foundation for Cancer Research. Carol herself is a breast cancer survivor and a Stehlin Foundation patient, and she undoubtedly deserves to have her name inscribed in the Hot Sauce Hall of Flame.

Yes, Mr. Chilehead has seen 'em all—Houston, Tucson—he's no stranger on the festival circuit. But let me tell you about my sojourn in Tucson, which is seared onto my memory.

Once upon a time, at the Tucson Botanical Gardens, while attending the Fiesta de los Chiles with my lovely Miranda, I had a close call with my own worst evisceration nightmare. I'd had one too many habañeros. Well, perhaps a few too many, and other fiery things besides. I was on holiday, you know? But since you're reading about this incident after the fact, you know that Mr. Chilehead still counts himself among the living.

It was a warm day. The cloudless sky was an impossible blue. We were wandering about, laughing and enjoying what the festival had to offer. It was a perfect day—I could not have invented a happier one. We sampled many spicy things. Our appetites were still capacious. Our palates were up for more challenges, however extreme.

We came upon a stall stacked with the most delectable-looking orange and red habañeros. They literally took our breath away. Plump and voluptuous, the peppers beguiled and seduced. Fondling them seemed only natural—they begged to be caressed, by the hand, the eye, the mind. Their auras were flaring; I could see them in my mind's eye, and the aura of a chile pepper is a wonderful sight. I bit into one, and it seemed remarkably tame, the mildest of volcanoes. I bit into a second.

This one was a real scorcher. I was whacked and flayed, but I survived. I should have stopped there, of course, but some deep-seated death wish overcame me and pushed me over the edge. I went for the gold. I was hit, and hard. My mouth was on fire, and my teeth felt as though they had been drilled into without benefit of anesthetic. I started to hyperventilate. I willed myself to remain calm, but it was hopeless. It was as though my very being had burst into flame. There was no way out. I had fallen into my very own ring of fire, and it burned, burned, burned.

I was lying on a funeral pyre without benefit of the last rites. I was one huge mouth with a tongue that was being incinerated from within. My heart was also in my mouth, where it had no right to be, and it was beating wildly. And all the while the heat was intensifying. I felt like Paul Atreides of Frank Herbert's *Dune* saga when the Reverend Mother of the Bene Gesserit sisterhood uses a pain-induction box to test whether he's human or animal. "Put your hand into the box. Your instinct will be to remove it. If you do so, you will die. First you will feel an itching, then a burning, then a crackling as the skin sloughs off . . ." Well, the habañero is a pain box. Can't stand it? Then you're a talking monkey. Are you a real man or woman? Grab a habañero/pain box and prove yourself.

I was a lump of moist dough shoved into a superhot oven and forgotten. It was as though shingles was raging through my entire organism. There was an inferno in my darkened forebrain, and sparks were flying everywhere. I knew that I would be utterly incinerated and only a carbon husk would remain. I felt kinship with William Hurt's character in Ken Russell's *Altered States*; seeking the godhead, he ingests a hallucinogenic substance during a tribal ritual, and a conflagration is ignited in his cerebral cortex.

Forgive me if I digress a moment. In the Amazon, chiles are sometimes used as an additive to hallucinogenic concoctions that tribal witchdoctors employ in healing rituals and vision quests. And certain chile peppers are utilized in ritual snuff mixtures containing various other hallucinogenic plants. Think of it: hallucinogens and chile peppers together! What a sucker punch! While the habañero is not a hallucinogen, its effect on the organism can be equally dramatic, traumatic, and unpredictable.

I was learning this the hard way. I felt myself falling. I'd experienced a similar sensation once before after drinking far too much dark rum on an empty stomach. As my descent towards some unknown sulfurous underworld accelerated, another powerful sensation gripped me: I was plummeting towards total blackout, supreme amnesia—death.

Somewhere far off, I heard Miranda's angelic voice: "Jimmy, wake up! Wake up, sweetness, you're gonna be okay!" I came to in a starched-white world. Unsparing light and artificial coolness—it felt like a morgue. Had I been catapulted through the chute? Was this it? Tunnel of light and all that? My internal fire had been extinguished. I was disoriented, and the sensation of having been toast not long before haunted me. The smell of smoking embers was still upon my medulla oblongata. I was lying in a hospital bed, far from the fray, wearing one of those horrible smocks with my backside hanging out. Miranda, a trained nurse, had taken my pulse at the festival site, found it to be weak, and called an ambulance. What had happened? Was it a little cardiac arrhythmia and a dead faint brought on by red-hot chile peppers? Or was it all those margaritas I had imbibed earlier? Who knows?

"Jimmy, welcome back," said Miranda. "I was so scared, but the doctor told me you're going to be okay." I felt like Lazarus—in the immortal words of Eliot's Prufrock, "I am Lazarus, come from the dead,/Come back to tell you all, I shall tell you all." I'd risen from the dead with a mission: I must warn chileheads everywhere, I must tell the cautionary tale of Mr. Chilehead's baptism by fire, Tucson-style. Mission accomplished. God bless.

I was in New York with Annie, a gentle soul. It was pre-9/11, when we could sleep at night without dreaming of it all crashing down around us. I'd been assigned by a Canadian art magazine to review the work of a major British artist who was showing in New York. We were staying at a nice downtown hotel with all the comforts and planned to eat at some of the city's best Indian restaurants—places like Jewel of India and Havati. I happily anticipated ordering dishes of searing vindaloo curry.

We also intended to visit some East Village bars, take the edge off with a few drinks, and soak up a little local color. At one such watering hole, we ran into Josh, an Aussie journalist I had met years earlier. We caught up, and then the conversation, as conversations among chileheads are wont to do, veered towards Painland. As we shared pepper lore, we were overheard by the bartender, a decent bloke, from whom we had ordered Bloody Marys. He invited us to sample his house specialty: habañero-infused vodka. Now, I have had pepper vodka before, and I've enjoyed it. Inferno is a good brand, and aptly named. But habañero vodka? This promised to be an eye-watering experience.

The first hot shot slid down the gullet leaving a little steam in its wake, but no harm done. Ditto shot two.

Then came the third, and the fourth. Annie had skipped breakfast and indulged in a big lunch. I love New York coffee-shop breakfasts, so I'd tucked into a hearty one and skipped lunch. Josh, as we discovered when we performed the post-mortem, had just had steak and fries. In other words, I was the only member of our trio drinking on an empty stomach, but I'd regarded this as a chile-tasting adventure, not an I-can-drink-you-under-the-table contest. By the time shot number five arrived, my palate was aflame and my heart was beating like a jackhammer. Sweat was running from my brow down the front of my Armani jacket and linen shirt like a proverbial waterfall. Lava flowed over my taste buds, and I felt eviscerated. I had been reckless. I fancied that the sensation in my gut paralleled the sensation a samurai experiences when performing a ritual self-disembowelment.

Annie and Josh, who had been models of composure—damn their stamina—were starting to look concerned. Robbie Robertson's "Somewhere Down the Crazy River" was playing in the background, and I followed the lyrics in my head as a means of holding on to my sanity. Then, after "I think I'll go down to see Madame X and let her read my mind," Robertson's voice stalled in my head. I was somehow on my feet and trotting towards the men's room. I just barely made it into a stall before I blacked out. The bartender—a good guy, even though he was obviously an ambassador from gin-joint hell—kept an eye on me while Annie rushed back to the hotel to get me fresh clothes. Every item of clothing I'd had on was fit to be burned.

The moral of Mr. Chilehead's story? I don't know if there is one. If there is, it's this: The chile pepper is opiate enough on its own, and mixing it with other intoxicants is pure folly. Peppers cooked in hashish oil? An interesting concept, but I think I'll pass. In any case, dear reader, I leave you to draw a line in the sand of your own recklessness.

Not long ago, I went to northern California to visit an artist whose paintings I loved. I was writing a catalog of her work for a San Francisco–area gallery. I had never mentioned my chile-pepper obsession to her; our conversations tended to be art-related, and the subject had never come up. A gifted abstractionist, Maria was also a gifted gardener. As my taxi rolled up to her door, I scanned the verdant landscape surrounding her house and was gratified to notice chile pods in the garden.

The artist, svelte and elegant, came out to greet me. "Maria, you are a sight for sore eyes!" I said, hugging her close.

"James! Welcome to my humble abode and garden."

"I didn't know you were a gardener, Maria. Do I see what I think I see?"

"You mean the peppers? Yes—I have Hungarian wax, long red cayenne, large red cherry, Thai hot, Mexibell, jalapeño, habañero, and a few others, inside and out. Let's have some lunch, and before we visit the studio I'll take you on a tour of my garden."

Well, we had a wonderful lunch, accented by fresh peppers of a quality and robustness to die for, and I knew I had arrived in paradise. During our garden tour, Maria explained to me that one needs to pamper hot peppers through germination because they originate in a tropical climate, but once they're established, they're fairly hardy. Chile peppers will survive in temperatures ranging from 45 to 85 degrees. "A little TLC goes a long way towards reaping heaven in Pepperland," said Maria.

I marveled at the spirit this talented painter had brought to the task of cultivating her little pepper oasis. "Yes, you've got to be vigilant. I must be sure the plants are well fertilized and protected from wind. They must be watered and exposed to lots of sunshine. The problem is the pests. The aphids are terrible. If you can control them, you can get a good stand." She went on to tell me that you can harvest chiles when they're still green, but they taste best once they've turned orange or red or yellow or brown.

Maria also emphasized the importance of pruning: "I prune my pepper plants religiously. Some five or six weeks before the first frost, I'll snip back the top branches and flowers. The strength will go to the existing peppers, which will mature faster. The yield is such that I have a supply of hot peppers all year long. I dry them in my windows. I freeze, roast, and crush them as well."

I learned an awful lot about raising chiles that day. A lot about art, too, and even more about a red-headed artist who is a genius at sowing and reaping crops of lovely peppers. Maria, too, deserves to have her name inscribed in the Hall of Flame.

I never met a burn I didn't like!

PYROMAN

I'd gone, covertly, to Montreal's West Island to learn what I could about a cabal of chile banditos, self-styled sauce aficionados and tireless proselytizers for the chile-pepper cause. Mr. Chilehead, as you know, has a powerful urge to patrol the territory looking for new hot sauces with higher and higher levels of heat; he is compelled to seek out like-minded citizens and purveyors of the heat. My mission that day was prompted by the following text, which I'd discovered while surfing the Net. How could I resist?

> The search was top secret. The quest, explicit: Find the ultimate hot sauce, excelling in both heat level and flavor. The results were inconclusive and the project ended. Or did it?
>
> In the hot-sauce underground (a place sought out by only the true masters of hot sauces), a group of hot-sauce fanatics quietly took matters into their own hands. They secretly hired a research and development professional to make a line of hot sauces to meet their

radical specifications. There were months of taste tests, market studies, and taste comparisons. Then finally, success was achieved!

But the mission didn't end there. The hot sauce fanatics wanted more. Why, they asked, couldn't we spice up ordinary foods into fiery masterpieces? Thus began a line of hot sauces, barbecue sauces, salsas, jellies/jams, even sweets. And still the quest continues, tapping all areas of the food spectrum.

We welcome you to explore our universe of fiery food products. You'll soon discover why the Underground Sauce Network is not your mainstream provider of hot sauce and hot-pepper products. Here in the underground, we know we'll bump into folks just like you who have been diligently searching for fiery food products that dare to go the distance.

I had to find that Underground Sauce Network and penetrate it. My mission took me to the suburb of Pointe Claire, to a bistro called Babaloo's. It was a sultry summer evening, perfect for a spicy encounter. With me was Stéphanie, a gifted artist and a budding chilehead. Our intention was to meet up with the chile-bandito cabal—they dubbed themselves the Spice Boys—and their "president," Marc Damato, the Benny Profane of chile pepperdom. This democratic if slightly warped group of fanatics takes over Babaloo's very Tuesday night with the avowed purpose of converting any nonchilehead who dares enter the place. They are also bent on celebrating their infatuation with the sauce that make all our lives hotter and more tolerable.

I'd arranged to hook up with the bartender, who had promised to introduce me to the group. As Stéphanie and I stepped through the bistro's door, however, we immediately noticed a large armoire with its doors propped open. Inside was an amazing assortment of hot sauces. We were waylaid. Our exclamations of delight caught the attention of the collection's proprietor, Patrick Downes, a core member of the Spice Boys. "So—you're into the sauce," he remarked. "Yes, very much so," I replied. "And Stéphanie here, my amanuensis for the evening, is too. We follow the heat, wherever it takes us."

After we'd made our introductions, I scanned the premises. The joint was jammed and abuzz with lively banter. Many customers were flushed and sweating copiously, and then I noticed that at the center of each table were bags, each holding a dozen or so bottles of sauce. We had obviously stumbled into the heart of Painland.

"So, Pat, can we taste your wares?" Generous and devout chilehead that he is, Pat replied, "By all means." We peered into the armoire. Pat's sauces were grouped according to their degree of heat. The mildest were on the bottom shelf, the medium-hot on the middle shelf, and some genuinely hot sauces occupied the uppermost berth. Among this assortment were four sauces I lacked, which instantly justified the trek to the West Island for me—and our visit had only begun. Pat offered to set up a plate for us. We eagerly accepted and watched as he uncorked bottles and poured little pools of sauce onto a large plate. It was a beautiful sight—Stéph the painter observed that the plate looked like a painter's palette.

There were 10 different sauces on the palette, from mild to incendiary. The hottest—Da' Bomb: The Final Answer—occupied the center spot. A bucket of barbecued chicken wings arrived, and we doused them in steak spice, squeezed lemon juice on them, and rolled them in sauce. We agreed that the Hottest Fucking Hot Sauce in the World failed to live up to its title; nevertheless, it was hot. We settled in for a long, warm evening.

Downes then introduced us to Marc Damato, panjandrum of the Spice Boys and a dyed-in-the-sauce chilehead. Damato was in San Francisco in the late 1980s when Dave Hirschkopf created Insanity and started his ascent of the Painland hierarchy, and he evinced a certain nostalgia for those halcyon days. The pain that Dave was peddling became central to Damato's existence. "When I visit my dentist," he confided, "I tell him to forgo the anesthetic. He cannot believe it. You see, I have been there, done that. Pain is my métier." This sentiment was heartily approved by all present.

It's interesting that a longtime Painland passport holder like Damato would also hold a doctorate in combustion physics. It could be that his knowledge of explosives protects him from spontaneously combusting while practicing hot-sauce rocket science. I pondered this as Damato generously prepared a plate for us of still rarer and hotter sauces. We swapped hot-sauce anecdotes until some peppers that Damato had recently brought back from China had their way with my vocal chords.

Downes and Damato then introduced us to Gilles Langlois, a gifted saucemeister who has created a number of sublime hot-sauce recipes. We sampled his Italian hot sauce—thick, savory, and scrumptious—which brought back memories of my dad's spaghetti sauce. Reaching into his sauce sack, Langlois withdrew a bottle of pickled habañeros and shyly offered them to the assembled chileheads. I popped one into my mouth. Ouch! But what a lovely slow blaze, intensifying as it rolled down my throat. Sheer excrescence of heat, but what a wonderful flavor. The lush liquid fire in that bottle proved to be the capstone of the evening. Langlois's culinary finesse fires up the Spice Boys legend, and the man surely belongs in the Hot Sauce Hall of Flame. I look forward to the day he starts marketing his products. The Spice Boys (and girls—there are several hot-sauce goddesses, such as Erika Johnson, among their ranks) are valorous chileheads, one and all. And their homegrown pepper community is remarkable, as are all such chile cabals, for its closeness, solidarity, and mighty love of all things hot. We bid our chilehead companions goodnight and left Babaloo's satisfied and enflamed. Network penetrated; mission accomplished.

Miranda and I found ourselves in New Orleans at carnival time. Carnival has been celebrated in the Big Orange and southward along the Gulf of Mexico for over 300 years, but each time I've attended, the proceedings seem saucier than ever. How is it possible? Likely because humanity's capacity for hedonism knows no limits. Furthermore, as any carnival-goer can attest, there is nothing else quite like Mardi Gras, and the chile pepper fits Mardi Gras hand in glove.

Some of my most cherished hot-sauce memories are set in the city's fabled French Quarter, so that's were we headed, checking into the Place d'Armes—a classic, casual, and supremely comfortable establishment. It's also the only hotel at Jackson Square. Comprised of nine beautifully restored eighteenth-century buildings surrounding a traditional flowering courtyard and patio with pool, the place is nicely situated, with Saint Louis Cathedral and Bourbon Street nearby.

We spent our first day sightseeing, strolling along the Mississippi River to the Aquarium of the Americas. Miranda had her fortune told by one of the city's many itinerant tarot card readers. "I see hot, very hot things in your future. I smell smoke! Be careful and watch what you eat!" she was instructed. Later, we happened in to an out-of-the-way bistro and ordered hot tamales—authentic Mexican hot and spicy tamales, beef rolled in cornmeal and seasoned with Cajun spice. Lord, they were hot!

Lovely, just lovely. The chef had been generous with the old habañeros.

The next night, Fat Tuesday, we each had a Sazerac, the bourbon-laced cocktail for which the city is (in)famous. After the first, we did what most wise people do: ordered another. Then we took to the street and entered a voyeur's dream: Bourbon Street was chock-full of beauteous and wantonly bared flesh. The balconies overhanging the thoroughfare were jammed with people; men leaned over the rails, trying to tempt passing women with fistfuls of shiny beads. Three or four masked men or women in red devil costumes wove through the crowd, handing out offerings. I made my way over to one of them and grabbed a few. The offerings were bottles. Upon closer inspection, I discovered that they were hot-sauce bottles! Squinting in the dim light, I read the label: "There is no telling how hot this sauce is. Reveler, beware! As time winds down towards the Witching Hour, this sauce heats up!" Miranda responded, "How very enticing."

When NOPD's finest commenced their mounted parade down Bourbon Street marking the official end to Mardi Gras, we headed back to the hotel to continue our celebration. I confess that we were already fairly sauced from imbibing a number of Sazeracs, but sampling the hot sauce—which was, in fact, not a hot sauce but an extract—seemed like a good idea at the time. I took a teaspoon. Suddenly, I wanted to dance; it was as though I'd been bitten by a tarantula. But my legs were paralyzed.

I could not speak. My vocal chords had somehow been shredded. My mouth was a gaping furnace inside my head. Sweat poured down my body like spring rain. My tongue was swollen. I was breathing far too rapidly. Miranda starting splashing beer on my face in a failed effort to diminish the heat. Then she covered my face with a cold towel and poured more beer on it.

It took me two days to recover. I was left with the vivid memory of the door to hell gaping wide in my brain. That was the fieriest Mardi Gras I have ever experienced—a true baptism by fire. Listen, folks, if a stranger on the street should happen to offer you a bottle of hot sauce, say, "Thanks, but no thanks. I have my own supply." If you don't, it could cost you your life.

I can say only in my own defense that I've known them all and survived to tell the tale.
MR. CHILEHEAD, WITH CHARACTERISTIC MODESTY

We've all heard hot-sauce stories over the years that non-chileheads might consider apocryphal. But the truth of the matter is that hot-sauce experimentation is an extreme pursuit, and it can be an extremely painful one. The purveyors of the stuff know this, of course, and they relish their diabolical reputations. The more fire they create, the more devotion they inspire, and the better they feel.

It seems that these days everyone and his great-aunt wants to concoct the hottest of the hot. Take The Source. At 7.1 million Scoville units, this Hades in a bottle is hazardous material. If not handled with the utmost respect, the contents of this tiny bottle of liquid hellfire will leave first-, second-, or even third-degree burns on your lips, tongue, mouth, throat, vocal chords, guts, and sphincter. Bear this in mind: A first-degree burn is like sunburn—it hurts, it reddens the skin, and after a few days it begins to heal. A second-degree burn causes wet blisters to develop, which can take two weeks to heal—if you're lucky. A third-degree burn penetrates the skin deeply, making it feel dry and hard and damaging nerves; surgery may be required.

The Source is the source of another of my vivid memory fragments. I first heard about the sauce from our good friends at Original Juan Market; they were marketing it strictly as a "food additive." Of course, I had to have a bottle, and when I got it I just couldn't leave it unopened. So then what happened, you ask?

When I opened The Source, a genie popped out and asked if I wished to remain alive. I said "Yes," and here I am today—alive and well. But it could easily have been otherwise. When the UPS truck pulled up to my door with the precious bottle, I was stirring an enormous pot of my favorite chile con carne. A propitious arrival. "How's the book coming?" the driver asked. He'd brought a heck of a lot of hot sauce to my door over the years, and I had told him that I was writing this book. "It's coming," I replied.

When he was safely out of the way, I put on my snow goggles and a pair of plastic gloves and opened The Source. Using the dropper attached to the cap, I let a single drop plop into the chile pot. "Just one?" I asked myself. "No, two. Hey, how incendiary could one drop be?" I added four more drops. Later in the day, I served myself a bowl of chile. The steam that rose from it seemed to promise the heat I was craving. I dipped a chunk of cornbread into the chile and popped it into my mouth. Whoa! Jeepers creepers, that was hellish hot! Great balls of fire! Good Lord Almighty! My mouth was on fire. Still, it was not a murderous order of heat. It was manageable. I could cope. A few cans of Guinness later, I was ready for my homemade habañero chocolate hot sauce with banana ice cream.

Okay, I know what you're thinking: I chickened out. When confronted with The Source, I didn't test the limits of my endurance. Well, you're right. I opted to remain among the living. However, it is comforting to know that if I ever have a change of heart in that regard, The Source is close at hand. What a way to go!

I was in New Mexico to see Site Santa Fe, the respected art carnival. And to eat. I happen to love the regional cuisine, with its hot and happy marriage of American, Spanish, Mexican, and cowboy influences. The chile pepper reigns supreme in Southwestern American cooking, and many agree that this cuisine is among the finest and fieriest in the country.

Santa Fe deserves its reputation as a center for fine dining, so I'm reluctant to name the restaurant in which the following rather unsavory incident transpired. Let's just say that there are some really great places to eat in town, including Geronimo's, which is located in a historic Canyon Road Adobe. Maria's is the perfect place to spend a romantic evening with your main squeeze, and it's home of the best margarita in Santa Fe. At Gabriel's, situated north of town near Camel Rock Casino, the prepared-at-your-table guacamole is simply to die for.

One day during my visit, a few of us Site Santa Fe participants—artists, critics, and curators who had known one another for years—converged on a certain establishment for lunch. We'd heard they served heavenly enchiladas, tortillas, and posole there. Placing our orders, we also asked for a bowl of chiles. Among our party was Artist X, a man notorious for his roving eye, who was new to Santa Fe and to hot chile peppers. Also on hand was Curator Y, from whom Artist X had stolen a cherished lover. X had recently apologized to Y for this transgression, but their presence still caused tension within the group.

We settled in for an amiable chat, but X had downed several margaritas and could not be restrained from discussing the plans he'd made with a "hot babe" he'd met earlier in the day. He then made the mistake of worrying aloud about the effect alcohol could have on his performance that evening. Y claimed to have a helpful suggestion for X, and, leaning over, whispered it into his ear.

I'd been observing all of this, but just then my attention was distracted by a couple of cowgirls at the next table.

Shortly afterwards, I noticed that X was missing from the table. Then I heard screaming. It was horrible —howls of agony tapering off into abject whimpers. Y got up to leave. "Where's X?" I asked. "Is that him howling?" Replied Y, "Well it might be. I told him that I'd heard that rubbing raw chiles on your penis and testicles ahead of the event will make you last longer. I never thought he would actually try it. But you know X, always hot to trot. Too frisky for his own good. Stickman may now be stickless." Then he added, in an unconvincing tone, "How very, very sad."

So ends Mr. Chilehead's personal narrative, a series of painful and pleasurable recollections deriving from my ongoing pursuit of the flaming pepper. There are actually many more fragments of agony and ecstasy where that came from, but you get the picture. Now let's turn our attention to the touchy topic of suicide—sauce-assisted suicide, that is.

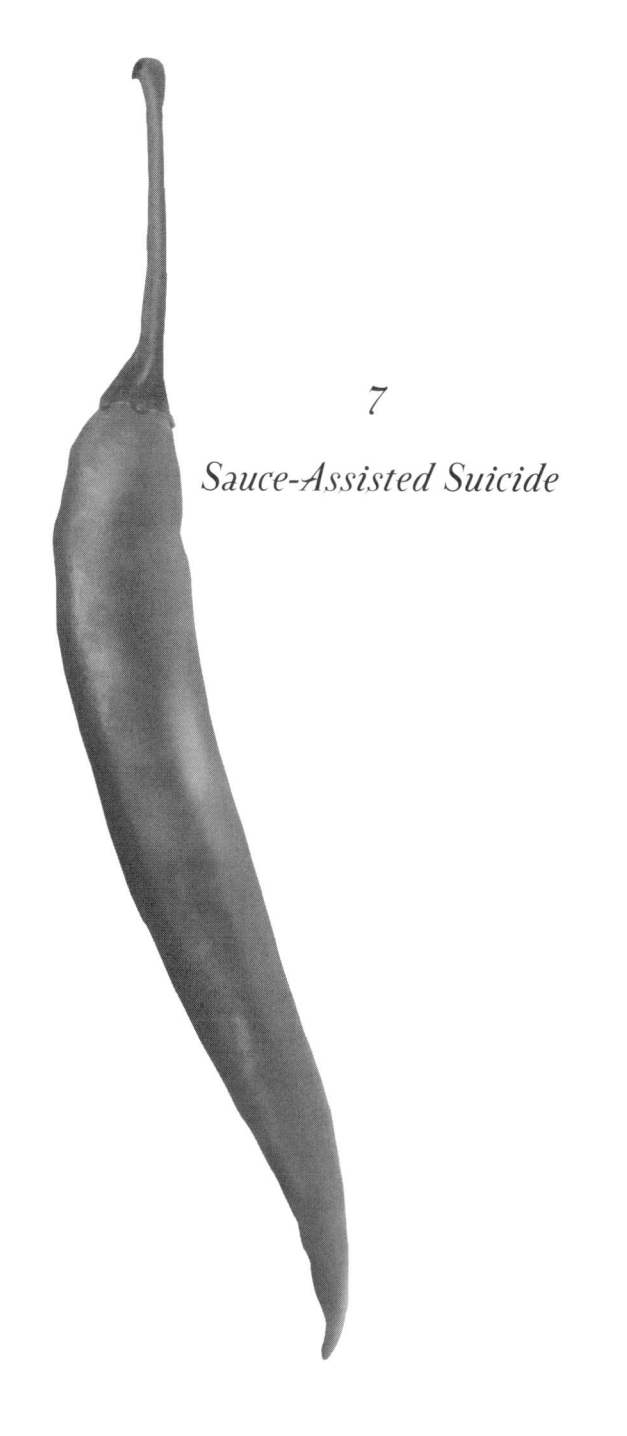

7
Sauce-Assisted Suicide

> *Ah, to be a gringo in Mexico with a bottle of Da' Bomb: The Final Answer—that is euthanasia.*
>
> ANONYMOUS CHILEHEAD
> (WITH APOLOGIES TO AMBROSE BIERCE)

Are you the sort of person who enjoys the sensation of having your tongue tattooed with chile-pepper juice and a knitting needle? Do you use Pure Cap as a lubricant? Do you dance a tarantella on the edge of a straight razor in order to trim your toenails? Hang out at the local nuclear plant in the hope that a little stray radioactivity will take the edge off? Fantasize about parachute jumping without a rip cord? Well, then you're probably the sort of individual who, when you read "Warning: Use this product only a single drop at a time. Not for people with heart or respiratory problems" on the side of a sauce bottle, promptly uncorks the stuff and pours it down your gullet like a Corona beer.

As peppers multiply like the frisky rabbit fruits they are throughout the verdant acreage of America and around the globe, the uses to which they are put proliferate as well. People everywhere are becoming enthralled with the idea of testing their tolerance for pain with chiles. The fiery fruits have spawned an entire subculture bent on self-immolation and undertaking games of culinary brinkmanship.

Chileheads also seem drawn to the spectacle of others in the throes of chile-pepper agony. They long to compare notes on heat levels and survivor ratios. The human tasting panel initiated in 1912 and called the Scoville Organoleptic Test was eventually disbanded and replaced by machines, but legions of brave chileheads out there have taken it upon themselves to duplicate the test. Whole congregations of chileheads have been created for this purpose. Then there is the suicidal hot-sauce-consumer fringe—and we could all name a few who fit into that category, couldn't we?

The heat rush that follows hard upon the ingestion of wickedly hot chiles presents the perfect opportunity for duelists of all stripes. When blood rushes to your abdomen and your body temperature rises; when you start to perspire like a running tap; when your heart and breathing rates increase; when your muscles start to ache with the exertion of the experience, then you want a challenge. You want to compete with another chilehead to see who survives and who winds up in a shuddering heap on the sawdust-strewn floor of the saloon. Just imagine it. There you are, in a heated contest with an earnest rival, on the verge of hyperventilating, lips in rictus mode and mouth afire, muscles aching, hanging from the cliff face by your fingertips . . . and—nirvana! Heaps of pleasure and the promise of still more to come. You have achieved the so-called chile high.

We humans have an inherent need for danger, and capsaicin delivers big-time. Chile peppers prey on our sense of adventure, on our need to test the limits and existing definitions of pain—or die trying. Did you watch *Survivor Thailand* and wish you could have been the contestant who had to eat the insects? Do you make dates with Russian women on the Internet? Are you a rock climber? Do you love fast cars, roller coasters, and so forth? Then the wild ride that the chile pepper offers is tailor-made for you.

Sauce-assisted suicide—or accidental demise, depending on the circumstances and one's frame of mind—is all a matter of capsaicin, that divinity among chemicals. Capsaicin is so hot that a single drop diluted in 100,000 drops of water blisters the tongue. In its pure form, it is a white powder with a Scoville heat rating of approximately 16 million units—the effects of which on the organism are likely akin to those outlined by Arthur Machen in his transmogrification masterpiece of supernatural horror, *Novel of the White Powder*. Capsaicinoids are located mainly in the pepper's placenta. Which seems appropriate, when you think about it. The placenta. Hmmm.

The seeds are packed closely against the ribs, which share the heat. And capsaicinoids are disseminated throughout the flesh of the fruit. Thus, any one part of the same pepper may be hotter or milder than another part. You can reduce a chile pepper's heat by removing its ribs and seeds. You must wear gloves while doing so, especially when handling the blessed habañero. Forgo the gloves only if you're contemplating a nasty act and want to eliminate the problem of telltale fingerprints.

Capsaicin, among scientific types, is also known as N-vanillyl-8-methyl-6-(E)-noneamide. Now there's a mouthful. It is without question the most robust and pungent of the group of compounds called capsaicinoids. Capsaicin and di-hydrocapsaicin together constitute 80 to 90 percent of the capsaicinoids found in peppers. A chile pepper's capsaicinoid content is measured in parts per million. The parts per million are then converted into Scoville units, the industry standard for measuring a pepper's wallop. One part per million is equivalent to 15 Scoville units.

The Scoville scale climbs from a very mild level to the upper stratosphere of Painland. Bell peppers have zero Scoville units; they are the poorest of peppers; they have no heat whatsoever. The habañero, however, is fraught, registering an unholy 200,000 to 300,000 units. The red savina habañero—at 577,000 Scoville units—once topped the scale, but now some genetically engineered peppers have eclipsed it.

Oleoresin capsicum, a concentrated extract of hot peppers, is a natural foodstuff. The extraction is performed like this: hexane, an organic solvent, is forced through dried, ground hot peppers, yielding a liquid; the liquid is then processed to remove the solvent. The substance that remains consists of the natural oils, color, and heat (capsaicinoids) of the hot peppers. On the Scoville scale, the extract measures anywhere between 430,000 and 2 million units.

Those of us who partake of hot peppers at every meal—the kind that rocket to the top of the Scoville charts—develop a tolerance that we tend to exaggerate when engaged in duels with our bold confrères. And these feats of one-up-personship just wouldn't be satisfying if the participants weren't good poker players. There's fun to be had here, but remember that in a poker game of this nature, the stakes are very high. The suicidal can accomplish their ends with relative ease; all other chileheads must resist carrying things too far and doing something truly silly. The creator of the aforementioned red savina habañero has had the pepper tested, and it contains over 577,000 Scoville units—*The Guinness Book of World Records* lists it as the hottest chile pepper in the world. Bite into a few of those, and your earthly woes will soon be over, my friend.

For those fringe chileheads who can't help but be drawn to the notion of sauce-assisted suicide, I'll toy with it for a while. Let's climb the Scoville scale and take a closer look at the culprits that occupy the top spots. But first understand that I absolve myself of blame for any rash acts you may be inspired to commit. Mr. Chilehead must insist that you heed this disclaimer. There can be no exceptions. I will not be responsible for any foolhardiness.

The Source

At 7.1 million Scoville units, this stuff is death in a bottle. "All things, good or bad, are driven by energy"— that's the message on the label, and it's pretty clear.

Pretty understated, too, if you consider all those Scovilles. The energy packed into The Source can certainly transport you to the dark side of Painland, if that's your schtick. The Source is a miniscule nuke that will raise a mushroom cloud inside your head.

One Million Scoville Units Concentrated Pepper Extract

Advertised as a "food additive only" and not a condiment, this extract is the first to be sold in a five- ounce bottle. It's pure, high-grade oleoresin capsicum and guaranteed to be 1 million Scovilles. Furthermore, it's been certified by high performance liquid chromatography (HPLC), a process that measures capsaicinoids in parts per million and converts the measurement to Scovilles. Retailers of this extract post warnings like "Keep away from children (not a joke or marketing hype)." This stuff is better than a hand grenade.

Da' Bomb: The Final Answer

The label reads "Great cooking ingredient for sauces, soups, and stews. Also strips waxed floors and removes driveway grease stains." And it bears the following warning: "Use this product one drop at a time. Keep away from eyes, pets, and children. Not for people with heart or respiratory problems." The suicidal need look no further. Here are a couple of typical retailer comments on Da' Bomb: "This one is almost twice as hot as the one I used to say was the hottest I have in my catalog!"; "This sauce is going to kill you. So hot, you should have someone nearby ready to dial 911 when you taste it." Final Answer, to be sure: this sauce packs 1.5 million Scoville units! To put this into some kind of perspective, consider that the jalapeño measures 5 million units, and the hottest pepper of them all, the habañero, measures only about 300,000. Taster Bob Nelson posted this testimonial on FireGirl.com: The "primary use" for The Final Answer "*must* be to start the barbecue. Pour it on the charcoal and *whoosh*, it bursts into flame! I can't imagine *any* culinary function to anything so hot, but maybe some people would refer to me as a 'wuss.'"

357 Mad Dog Hot Sauce

Sauce manufacturers point out that if a hot sauce is hotter than a pepper au naturel, then they cannot legally call it a hot sauce. They must label it a "food additive." Weighing in at 357,000 Scoville units, 357 Mad Dog is just under the legal limit to be called a sauce. Technically, then, it is perhaps the hottest true hot sauce in the world. It's a rabid, mad mongrel of a sauce.

Blair's 2 a.m., 3 a.m., 4 a.m., 5 a.m. Private Reserve Pepper Extracts

These miracles of the sauce-maker's art relentlessly push heat levels to the upper reaches of Painland—1.5 to 2 million Scoville units. Lethal, just lethal. All bottles are proudly and lovingly signed and numbered. Check out the disclaimer on FireGirl.com: "If you purchase the product known as Blair's 3 a.m. Reserve, you hereby acknowledge the intense heat factor of this product and the element of danger if misused. Blair's 3 a.m. Reserve is over 100 times hotter than a jalapeño pepper and is a complex blend of fresh peppers and extracts. This product is not a sauce but a food additive and should be used only as such. Furthermore, is should be clearly understood that Blair's 3 a.m. Reserve is used strictly at the purchaser's risk. Purchaser hereby releases Gardner Resources, Inc. (the manufacturer) and FireGirl, Inc. (the seller) from all liability, indemnifies and holds harmless Gardner Resources, Inc. and FireGirl, Inc. with respect to any claims of damages or injuries resulting from the use, consumption, ingestion, and/or contact with respect to Blair's 3 a.m. Reserve." The site also posts the remarks of a customer named Darren, who claims to have tested the sauce by adding a drop to a gallon of chile. Even at that dilution, it was spicy. Darren pushed ahead with his experiment and discovered that three drops was optimal—"Very, very spicy and very good."

Mad Dog's Revenge Pepper Extract
This stuff, measuring 1 million units on the Scoville scale, is 450 times hotter than Tabasco. Hard to believe, I grant you, but there it is. Twelve pounds of peppers go into each two-ounce bottle. This habañero extract is one of the purest available. Chileheads agree that it tastes just like a habañero.

Say you scan the foregoing list of suicide assisters, select one that particularly strikes your fancy, procure it, get your affairs in final order, ingest a lethal dose, and . . .

have a sudden change of heart. You're just not ready for the big exit. What to do? If you feel yourself to be in true jeopardy, call 911. As you await the paramedics, try to slow your breathing. And don't bite your tongue, or the paramedics might think that you're having an epileptic seizure and give you the wrong medication. Remain calm, if you can. Think of yourself as a self-styled *Titanic* ramming the iceberg rather than the sizzling mess of cinder-riven pottage that you are. Then, if you can manage it, try one of the following home remedies (adapted from *The Chilehead Survivors' Guide*, an undated and unpaginated publication).

Drink a tall glass of cold milk. (Do not, as I emphasized earlier, drink water, because it merely spreads the heat around.) Take a big sip, roll the milk around in your mouth, over your tongue, and swallow hard. Repeat several times. The temperature in your mouth/furnace will slowly and mercifully decrease. Other dairy products, such as yogurt and ice cream, may also do the trick.

Starchy foods, like bread and potatoes, won't dissolve the capsaicin, but they will carry a certain amount of it down the throat. White rice works the same way—the Chinese use it for this very purpose. Alternatively, you could try drinking tomato juice or sucking on a fresh lemon or lime. But beer, and lots of it, is perhaps the remedy of choice: it both washes down the searing capsaicin and causes you to forget about the foolish behavior that landed you in this predicament in the first place.

Sail forth, fellow chilehead voyagers! Don't sign off just yet—new chile adventures still await you. Voyage to your outer limits and see what's there. But don't fall off the edge of your world. And try to stay just this side of the pearly gates, okay?

8

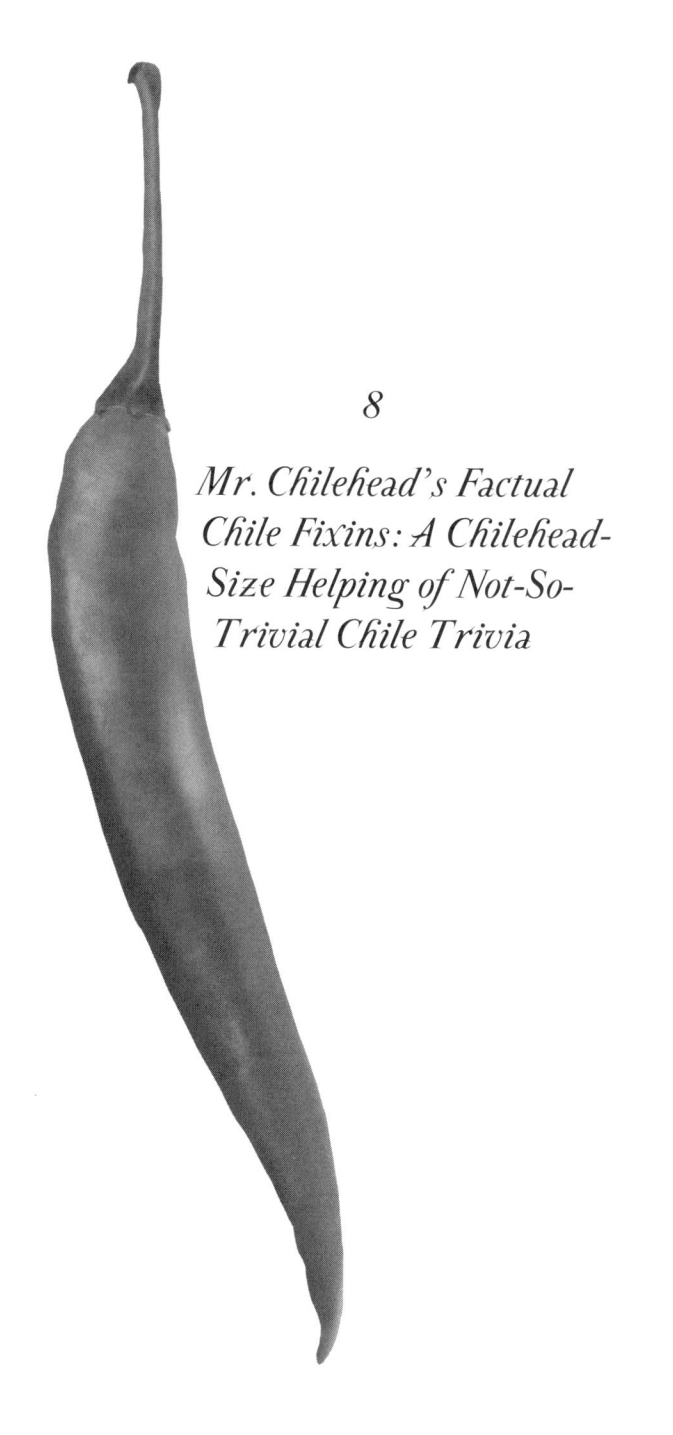

Mr. Chilehead's Factual Chile Fixins: A Chilehead-Size Helping of Not-So-Trivial Chile Trivia

122 MR. CHILEHEAD

> *Chile, Chile, Chile,*
> *We thank thee for this food and the Spice you bring,*
> *We thank thee for the Journey that thy Heat will launch,*
> *We thank thee for the Vision that thy Scovilles reveal.*
> *As ends this day, so shall the next,*
> *And so, sweet Chile, guide me to Enlightenment.*
>
> TRANSCENDENTAL CAPSAICINOPHILIC SOCIETY,
> "EVENING CHANT"

Being Mr. Chilehead means being a willing magnet and effective sponge for all sorts of information concerning chile peppers. And this information can be very useful. For instance, should I want to put together a chile trivia quiz or write a book like this one, I know I'll have no trouble accessing a wealth of exotic, unlikely, and downright dumbfounding chile data. It gives me great pleasure to share some of the informational gems that I've unearthed with you, my fellow chileheads. So kick back and allow me to present you with a compendium of coruscating data that's spinning around my chile-addled head like a rosy aureole of cayenne peppers in a wreath of pepperhead stew.

- The word *capsicum* derives from the Greek *kapto*, which literally means "to bite."

- In astrology, the capsicum falls under the dominion of Mars, ancient god of war.
- The word *chiltepin* stems from the Náhuatl dialect of the Aztec language. It was the name given to one of the earliest-known chile varieties and is thought to be a combination of the words "chile" and "tecpintl"; the combination translates as "flea chile," which references the bite of the chile pepper.
- Chiles were an integral part of the diets of the Incan, Olmec, Toltec, Mayan, and Aztec civilizations. There is evidence to show that the Aztecs used chile in almost every dish, laying the foundation for modern Mexican cuisine.
- One out of every four people in the world eats chiles; that is, 25 percent of the world's population are chile eaters.
- A fresh chile contains twice the vitamin C of any citrus fruit. Its vitamin A content exceeds the recommended daily requirement; it has high levels of vitamin E; it's loaded with calcium, iron, potassium, and beta-carotene.
- The chiles grown today in North America evolved from an ancient variety indigenous to Bolivia and Peru.
- It is believed that chile peppers made their first appearance in Central Mexico, in about 7000 B.C.
- The first chiles consumed were harvested from wild plants. Indigenous peoples raised chiles between 5200 and 3400 B.C., which makes chiles one of the oldest cultivated crops in the Americas.

- By the time the Spanish arrived in Mexico, Aztec plant breeders had already developed dozens of varieties of chile peppers. These were the antecedents of the varieties found in Mexico today.
- In the mid-1800s, an American soldier who had fought in the Mexican War returned to his native Louisiana with chile seeds from the Mexican state of Tabasco. The variety of peppers he grew from these seeds is now used to make Tabasco Sauce.
- The genus *capsicum* is a member of the nightshade family, which includes tomatoes, potatoes, tobacco, and petunias.
- In certain climatic conditions, chile-pepper plants flourish as a perennial shrub; a chile may live for 10 years or more in the tropics (in central South America, for example), but in other zones it's cultivated as an annual.
- New Mexico's official state vegetables are the chile and the frijole (pinto bean).
- Hatch, New Mexico, is known as the "Green Chile Capital of the World."
- "Chile" or "chili?" Debates about the correct spelling are heated. "Chile" is the Spanish adaptation of "chili," the Aztec designation for the pod. Nowadays, "chili" denotes a popular savory dish—a combination of beans, meat (if desired), and lots of pungent chile peppers.
- "Red or green?" Many hold that this is the most commonly asked question in all of New Mexico. "Which is hotter today?" may be the best response.

If you can't decide, order it "Christmas," the local way of saying "both red and green."
- Texas has two official peppers, the jalapeño and the chiltepin; both are used to make the official state dish: chile.
- A Japanese company has found a spicy way to keep mice from chewing up fiber-optic cables. Sumitomo Electric Industries, a big manufacturer of electrical wiring, has produced cable coated in synthetic hot pepper. Mice, apparently, have a strong aversion to hot pepper.
- A "cheechako" is an inexperienced chile-chomper. A "chilehead," of course, is the very opposite—Mr. Chilehead is a strong believer in the maxim, "The hotter the chile, the better the head."
- Chile peppers were once traded as common currency.
- Armando Martillance holds the record for eating the most chiles in a three-minute period: 500. On May 28, 2000, Martillance performed this astonishing feat at the annual Magayan Festival, held in the Philippines. The chiles used for the competition were capsicum frutescens, which are among the world's hottest peppers (this fascinating fact is courtesy of *The Guinness Book of World Records*, via my researcher— my 11-year-old son—who just ran into my study with the latest edition open to the relevant page).
- Chile flashes bear a remarkable resemblance to hot flashes, except that they're self-induced and non-gender-specific.

- To chileheads, a "hot date" is an assignation for a chile fix at a favorite Mexican restaurant.
- New Mexico's official "heat wave" takes place between August and October, when chiles are harvested and roasted.
- "Hotluck" is a potluck dinner featuring chile dishes.
- Hungarian scientist Albert Szent-Gyorgyi extracted vitamin C in significant quantities for the first time from the chile pepper. In 1937, he was awarded the Nobel Prize for his efforts.
- Paul Bosland—aka Chileman—renowned professor of horticulture at New Mexico State and founder of the Chile Pepper Institute, grows more than 1,000 different varieties of the pod each year in his on-campus test plots and greenhouses.
- Emma Jean Cervantes has been dubbed "New Mexico's First Lady of Chile Production." Her Cervantes Enterprises, located in Vado, south of Las Cruces, is one the state's largest chile-growing operations.
- Generally speaking, the smaller the chile, the hotter it is—and the happier the chilehead.
- Mixing cayenne pepper into chickens' drinking water makes the birds lay more eggs. Maybe the stuff warms up their nether regions ...
- Here's a great remedy for a sore throat: add habañero powder to the water you're heating for your instant cocoa. Try it and be cured!
- A pinch of habañero flakes in your Bloody Mary will set your world on fire.

- Chilate is a Salvadoran drink of ground corn simmered with malagueta chile, which is similar to the tabasco chile.
- In his book *Peppers: A Story of Hot Pursuits*, Amal Naj writes, "According to government records maintained during the British rule [in India], Hyderabad, now the capital of Andhra, had the highest annual consumption of green and red chiles in the country." Naj goes on to explain that the poor did most of this consuming. "Hot peppers didn't figure much in the foods of the rich and the nobility, who preferred black pepper, cardamom, and saffron and other exotic spices of the time. The poor couldn't afford these aromatic spices and relied instead on hot peppers" (211).
- The chile pepper has now replaced salt as the world's most frequently used seasoning and condiment.
- According to Dave DeWitt and Nancy Gerlach in *The Whole Chile Pepper Book,* "A Peruvian expression, 'gringo huanuchi,' describes the rocoto chile: It's hot enough to kill a gringo—a blond or Anglo person".
- Fuentes y Guzmán wrote in 1690 that those who regularly consumed red pepper were protected against poison.
- Throughout the world, one of the most common uses of the chile pepper is fumigation; when burned, the chile kills vermin.
- "Chile is used as an amulet, probably because of its well-known protective pharmacological properties, and in religious ceremonies, witchcraft, and conjuring; its fiery potency is considered a powerful means

to any end," claims Beatrice Roeder in *Chicano Folk Medicine from Los Angeles*.

- Ottawa-based Chilly Chiles, in operation since 1993, was the first company in Canada to specialize in fiery fare. Owners Rob Myers and Alison Steele-Myers have also made Chilly Chiles the country's first fiery-food mail order firm. Check out their exceptional catalog and Web site.
- Brazilian folk healers who concoct herbal remedies containing chile peppers are called "pimentologos."
- Native peoples once tied ristras—strings of red chile pods—to their canoes to ward off evil forces lurking beneath the water's surface; nowadays, ristras are commonly used in households as symbols of welcome.
- The Indians of Mexico's Sonoran Desert believe that chile eaters are protected against a sorcerer's bad spell; those who refuse to eat chiles run the risk of being suspected of sorcery themselves.
- On the Internet, Dave DeWitt mentions his friend Lorenzo Fritz, who travels regularly to South America to live with Native peoples and collect chile information, which he relays to DeWitt. The Aymara Indians of Bolivia, writes DeWitt, "conduct a spiritual cleansing ritual in which a mixture of various herbs, flowers, and *locoto* chile (*Capsicum pubescens*) are placed in a pail of boiling water. The subject sits on a stool nearby, and a blanket is placed over him and the pail to form a mini-sauna. Lorenzo, who observed the ceremony, noted: 'This exercise is said to be an

exorcism for *malas energías*, or bad energies (www.fiery-foods.com/dave/mythology.html).'"
- The Tijuana Flats Burrito Company offers over 3,500 hot sauces for sale online. The company is also responsible for Smack My Ass and Call Me Sally of the Slap Heard Around the World hot-sauce line—truly incendiary stuff.
- "A peculiar effect of capsicum is worth mentioning. In Mexico the people are very fond of it, and their bodies get thoroughly saturated with it, and if one of them happens to die on the prairie the vultures will not touch the body on account of its being so impregnated with the capsicum" (*The Standard Guide to Non-Poisonous Herbal Medicine*, quoted in Kloss).
- A new Internet cult has emerged called the Transcendental Capsaicinophilic Society. On their Web site (from which this chapter's epigraph has been taken), cult founders declare their devotion to "the worship of all Chiles," pledge their "life-long dedication to Chile consumption," and admit that they enjoy "making fun of people who just can't take that spicy food." They invite all like-minded individuals to "join our swelling ranks" (www.io.com/~m101/tcs).

And with this delightful bit of lunacy from the good chileheads at TCS, we conclude our brief foray into chile trivia. Now, how about dipping into a little chile erotomania?

9

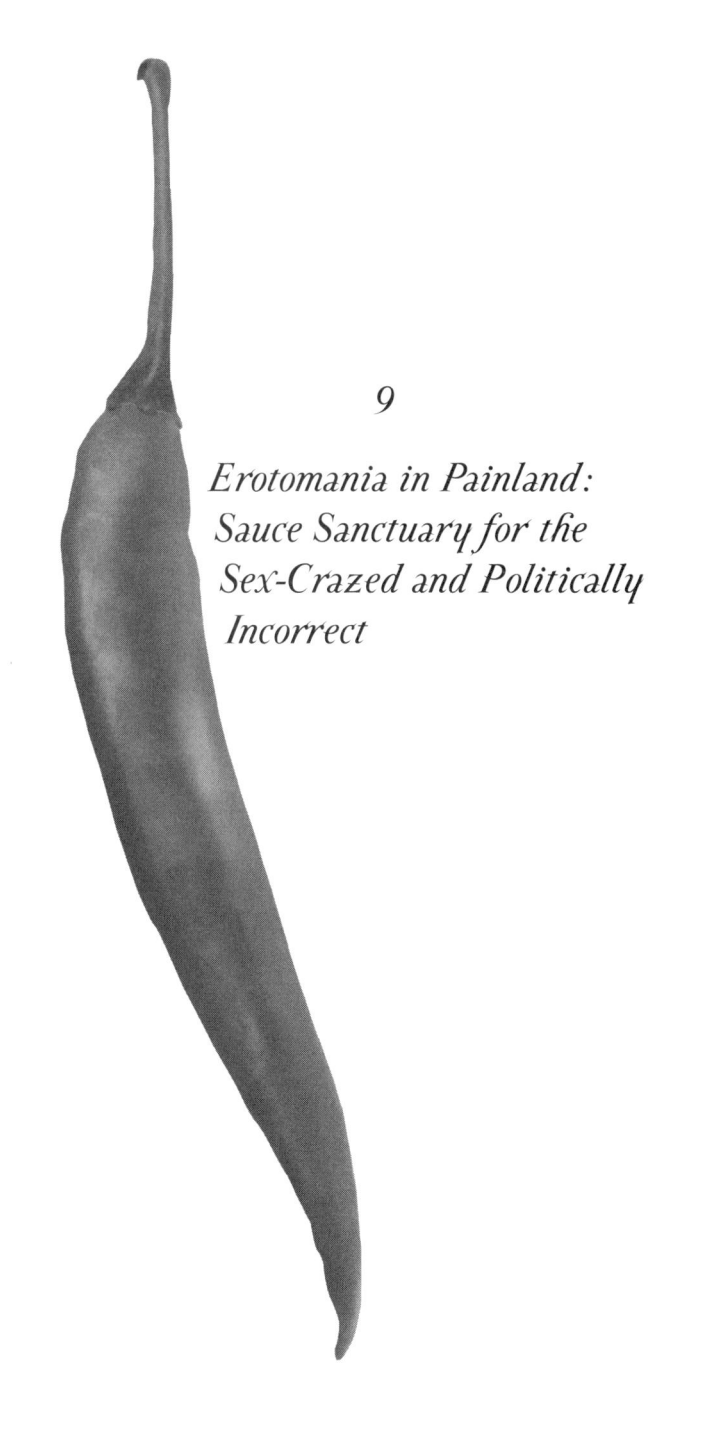

Erotomania in Painland: Sauce Sanctuary for the Sex-Crazed and Politically Incorrect

> *I feel the habañero heat*
> *The habañero heat between me and you.*
>
> PRINCE (PARAPHRASED)

I am proud to begin this final chapter of our odyssey by introducing to you some of my closest friends. But be warned! These lovely, erotic creatures are highly inflammatory! Handle with care, and don asbestos (or at least wear latex gloves) if you dare. Are you up to it? These divinities will sorely test your manhood.

Ms. Red Savina Habañero

This pepper was once listed in *The Guinness Book of World Records* as the world's hottest pepper. She is sought-after. She is expensive, definitely the exotic star of the chile-pepper escort service to hell. She is a delectable Initiatrix and a sultry forbidden fruit who harbors more than 5 million Scoville units. Use wisely, if you want to stay alive, in salsas and other concoctions. On fire, all the time. Prepare to be flayed within a wee inch of your life.

Ms. Orange Habañero

World renowned for her incendiary heat, the divine Ms. Orange has gorgeous thin walls and a captivating aphrodisiac fruity flavor. A princess among fruits, she's roundish or heart shape. She is two inches long, ranging in color from orange sherbet to pistachio. She's justly considered the hottest domesticated chile in the world—her ample measurements in Scoville units range from 100,000 to 500,000. Arguably, she's the prettiest patrician-featured pepper of them all, and her fulsome shape hints at the fires awaiting you inside. This Mistress of Secrets can be a real dominatrix, so watch yourself. But do submit, even if you are not by nature a submissive. She'll make you pay for it.

Savor her flavor: it starts out all floral and fruity and seemingly tame; then the heat infusion comes on fast, shooting up your nostrils like cocaine or wasabi. The scent and the flavor are absolutely unforgettable.

In Peru, habañeros are aptly nicknamed "levanta muertos," or "raise the dead." They can raise you straight up, in more than one sense, and send you over the edge. Great for a last-minute Lazarus routine. If you're a wuss bag, then clear the area. But if you can stand the punishment, stick around. This naughty number flirts energetically with all manner of other companions, but she marries best with fruits—such as mango, pineapple, and papaya—whose inherent and luscious ethos of fruitiness are accentuated by the arresting perfume-like overtones of the habañero clan.

Ms. Red Cayenne
This mature redhead has a deep, sensuous red complexion and lots of sultry glamour. She is about six inches long (but she can be shorter or longer), and she's slender, even

svelte, in profile. Ms. Red is pretty hot, and pretty damn enticing, too, weighing in at a pleasing 30,000 to 50,000 Scoville units.

Used principally in powdered form, she is a fine source of primordial heat. When you slowly suck her lovely contours like the toes of a loved one, your mouth and lips catch fire. Compatible with Cajun cooking, this hot number may also be consumed whole—whoa!—in various Chinese and other dishes. Go easy, though, and make sure your stamina is up. You'll need it. You don't want to disappoint with a mediocre performance, now do you?

Ms. Green Cayenne
This long-legged yet graceful gamine of a green chile grew up mainly in India and Asia; she's featured in Indian, Indonesian, and Pakistani cuisines. Ms. Green, I must tell you, is less mature—and a little cooler and more reserved, at 30,000 to 40,000 Scoville units—than Ms. Red. Still, she has her charms, and her legion of admirers. She'll make you put up *and* shut up.

Ms. Serrano
A native of Mexico and the American Southwest, this beauty is widely believed to be one of the most fetching chiles of them all. She's adorable in either her red or her green silken dress. Petite, skinny, and pointy, but always elegant in her demeanor, she is about five times hotter—with a Scoville rating that exceeds 20,000—than Mlle.

Jalapeño. Because you don't have to peel off this little thin-skinned beauty's dress before tasting, she's easy to use in salsas. A real firecracker, her taste is fresh, tart, and always biting. She has a delayed fuse, so be careful how much you consume when you start in on her!

Mlle. Jalapeño
This comely miss never fails to make my heart beat faster as I squeeze her rack at the produce market. Plump and pleasing, she causes my palms to sweat, and I occasionally get all teary-eyed and aroused when I catch sight of her across a crowded room in the principality of Painland. Mlle. Jalapeño possesses a distinctive and pungent perfume. With her thick, fleshy walls, she is voluptuous and always very flavorful. It's so sad when she starts to wrinkle. This fetching chile (measuring 2,500 to 5,000 Scoville units) is a tidy two to three inches long, wider at the stem end, with an endearing blunt, nipple-like tip. In any season, she's a pleasure to caress, dote upon, and consume. Her dark-green skin is sleek, shiny, and firm to the touch. She's bodacious and refined. This beguiling maiden arguably possesses the richest flavor of all the small chiles. She lives to be made into salsa, stuffed as an appetizer, or munched whole by parched and waiting-to-be-scorched pepper-crazed suitors like yours truly. If that Habañero vixen hadn't monopolized Mr. Chilehead's affections so thoroughly, then this lovely thing would be his main squeeze.

I invite you to applaud these lovely guests at the pajama party I've thrown for all you chileheads and chileheads-in-the-making. I must confess that I love nothing more than to dance salsa or tango with them all together or individually and sup on all their tender bodies together or individually, if you catch my drift. And now that I've put you in the mood, let's explore the erotic dimension of Painland in more depth.

Americans are both irreverent and inventive. That's their rep. Extensive areas of their popular culture have a no-holds-barred character; they celebrate sarcasm, extreme behavior, and all sorts of naughtiness for its own sake. Such impulses have found an ideal medium for expression in the hot-sauce label. The mad hankering of Americans for all things hot, hotter, hottest, though seemingly unfettered, is succinctly contained in those small paper rectangles that are glued to the sides of hot-sauce bottles.

We New World chileheads are bent on taking a wild, raunchy ride across the night side of Painland, and the purveyors of the sauce furnish us with road signs for our journey. They command their label makers to assume X-rated personas, to suggest to us that a Painland boudoir is a far better place to consume hot sauce than the kitchen table ever was. A lust for the heat inflames their creative minds, producing a cheerful obscenity, which, in turn, they channel into their hot-sauce labels—or "politically incorrects," as they are known in the industry.

Only an American could devise a sauce bottle labeled "Ain't Milk" depicting the adorable Monica sporting an "ain't milk" moustache. You don't have to be a chilehead to understand the reference to Slick Willie and his unstatesman-like comportment . . . it's clearly his recently ejaculated semen smeared above her fulsome red lips. Then there's Monica's Down on Your Knees Hot Sauce. On the label we see a busty, beret-sporting Monica on her knees with her panties around her ankles, wearing a toothy grin. The text reads, "Be prepared! Put on your kneepads. Ask Monica. This hot, sweet sauce will bring you to your knees! Orally ingest a good dose of this spicy blend of hot peppers, mustard and honey (the elixir of the *Gods*) Douse liberally on your favorite tube steak, wiener, hot dog, sausage or whatever you like. Enjoy Monica's sultry pleasure." It requires sheer bravura and a high vulgarity threshold to come up with this stuff.

These days, there are more and more such labels—gloriously, gleefully, glibly in the gutter, and even downright obscene. Yet perhaps explicit, suggestive, provocative, or raunchy names are the appropriate complement to the innate heat of the habañero pepper sauces themselves. That heat gives rise to sexual heat, even if some of the more staid and shy among us choose to deny it. Hot sauces sweat sweet Eros, and this sweat, like kalas to a Tantrika, excites chileheads and eviscerates hypocrisy.

My buddy PyroMan, one of the foremost hot-sauce retailers in the United States and the brains behind pyro pepper.com, has admitted to me that "Most people (including me) are a bit skittish about actually reprinting the text from some of those bottles." He adds that there's many a sauce whose photo he won't post on his Web site either. Lots of sauce-bottle images are just too extreme, and they would likely be an affront to the politically correct customer. Rampant erotomania. As I've said, hot-sauce heat tends to kindle libidinal heat, releasing normally respectable people from their inhibitions. So we get a wee bit wild, a little carried away—do you, the affronted politically correct hot-sauce customer, really begrudge us our waywardness? Would you deny us a little fun? Hey, I grew up with two sisters, and I'm a devout feminist to boot, but I get a huge kick out of the more profane sauce labels—they speak to me, because when the habañero sheds its clothes in the slow cooker and the heat level rises, other things rise as well. If this is an uncomfortable truth, then it's also a very human truth.

The Pepper Girl Brand has released several notably hot sauces. One is Fifi's Nasty Little Secret Pineapple Jalapeño. Depicted on its label is a bodacious French maid tiptoeing out of a bedroom. A man's tie, a flower, and a couple of socks are strewn across the floor. The text reads: "She doesn't do windows, dust or mop. So what talents are bottled up inside this pretty little miss? You'll experience pure heated passion when she opens up to you and pours out her nasty little secret." Another of Pepper Girl's offerings is Sultan's Main Squeeze Passion Fruit Thai Pepper, a hot sauce whose label boasts a shapely harem girl and this text scenario: "Journey into the heart of the Casbah and be the Sultan's guest. He's far away on a traveling caravan and has summoned you to protect and console his harem for the night. But be warned! Stay away from the Sultan's favorite . . . The most tantalizing and passionate of all. There is a price to pay far beyond the realms of imagination for the Sultan's Main Squeeze." The price? Just try the sauce, without preconceptions.

The Los Angeles–based company XXX Rated Hot Sauces has devised a marketing strategy that links their Submission Hot Sauce with violent S&M practices—a brilliant ploy. The label includes the motto "Gagged, Bound and Blistered," and it features a cartoon-like rendering of a voluptuous woman with black tape covering her nipples being force-fed hot sauce through her gagged mouth while flames shoot forth from her anus. The profane folks at XXX have a number of other sauces in highly dubious taste, such as The Big Hot One: "Slide this baby between your lips and take a big swallow. Remember: Size does matter, especially in Scoville Units!" Brand New Asshole: "Hot Sauce that is guaranteed to rip you a new one!" Devil's Bitch: "Cum feel the flames of my bitchin' new hot sauce. You'll feel like the devil!" If you're really into S&M and have the stomach for it, check out the company's other labels at www.XXXratedhotsauces.com.

I recently came upon this delightful bit of zaniness on the Net: "Jeff's Formula 5 Hallucinogenic Hot Sauce 19-alarm Power! Formula 5's heat factor is off the scale. It will burn down your house and take your body with it.

You have been warned. We can assume no responsibility for spontaneous human combustion. Formula 5 has all the 'Triple X Erotic Take Me Now Yes'-ness you need. Just a teaspoon of Formula 5 will have you screaming ooooh yeah baby in no time even though there's no one else around. We know this much for sure: This hot number is not for the prudish! Are you saucy enough to swallow it all?"

Included with this posting were a few testimonials: "I thought I'd had the hottest hot sauce ever thought up when I ate Pedro's Full Commital Lifetime Madness Crazy Sauce. Let me tell you this, after trying Formula 5, I realized that Pedro is a marmalade-eating cookie-pusher and a full-blooded pansy. Pedro's sauce now tastes like applesauce to me and I won't even feed it to my parrot. Formula 5 is the only condiment that wakes me up in the morning and keeps me going all day. Why, I even put it in my coffee. I'm committed for life." That one from Angus, of Sudan, Texas. Here's one more, from Ed, of Okeene, Oklahoma: "Scrappy was our long-time family pet. Last week, we went to check on him and he was cold and hard—plumb dead. Well, he was such a good little doggy and we'd always said we'd go and get him stuffed if he passed on . . . we just didn't think it would be so soon. With me being on social security and Sally with her bad back, it's usually hand to mouth each month so we knew we'd have to do it ourselves with a book we got from the library. Sally said, 'Let's soak him in a tub full of Formula 5 to work as an embalming fluid.' I told her, 'Woman, that's the craziest bit of plumb foolishness I ever heard.' Don't you know she did it anyway and left him that way overnight to let it get soaked in good. The next morning we got up and Scrappy was running around like nothing had happened. I said, 'I'll be hogwashed.'"

The posting for this sauce powerful enough to raise the dead concluded with the following warning: "Formula 5 is a full-strength spicy adventure. It is not for tiny babies, small children, mamma's boys, sissy men, fragile princesses, or sick old ladies. In addition, pregnant women and people with heart conditions should not even stand near it except under the advice, direction, and immediate supervision of a doctor." Then this: "Attention! News Flash! Formula 5 Original Hot Sauce has been banned by the U.S. Government pending review. Sales have been stopped indefinitely. Please folks, stop calling and sending e-mail trying to get some. We can no longer manufacture the stuff in this country. Thanks for the offers, but the outrageous price bids you have been sending cannot be accepted. Also, as part of the court order, I can not disclose to anyone the directions on how to make it yourself, even though Formula 5 consists of 100% organically grown, all natural *legal* ingredients. And that's the truth. ©2000-2001 X. J. Scott, Red Barn Goat Farm (nonoctave.com)."

Now, is this a hoax? Perhaps. I have not been able to verify it. But, hoax or not, it says something about the X-rated hot-sauce mania that is rampaging like an STD across the nation. Chileheads feverishly engage in Eros-laden banter, and it infiltrates all discussion of hot sauce. Sexual heat seems endemic to Painland. It could well be that people with a penchant for sadomasochism and people who are fanatical about hot sauce are in fact the same people. Handcuffs? Whips? Add a little Pure Cap to the scenario and watch things shoot to a whole new level.

Here are the names of some of the raunchier sauces: Hottest Fuckin' Sauce, Colon Cleaner, Hard On, Hot 'n Horny, Red Rectum, Burning Bush, Screaming Sphincter, Rectal Rocket Fuel, Cock Flavored Soup Mix, Cock Sucker Sauce, Sir Fartalots, Pain and Suffering XXX-Rated, Butt Plug Relief, Hot Bitch at the Beach, Scorned Woman, Asburin, Ultimate Burn—and the list is getting longer all the time.

As we all know, there are a number of fascinating links between sex and politics. Hot sauce is one of them. Sauce makers have used their product labels as vehicles for ferocious political commentary just as they've used them to enflame the sensibilities of chilehead erotomaniacs. A great many hot sauces ridicule politicians, reflecting the deep skepticism with which Americans have come to regard career politicos. Victims of this trend include Bill Clinton, Al Gore, Dick Cheney, Ted Kennedy, George Bush—all the usual suspects. Mad as hell and can't take it anymore? Express your disgust with those elected to serve you by purchasing a bottle of Bush Sauce, Gore Bore Sauce, or Teddy's Hot Sauce. Or maybe murderous terrorists are the object of your fury. Go sauce shopping and pick up some Blown Away, or Bomb Laden—which, of course, bears Osama's hideous likeness. Or take the edge off with a bottle of Burn in Hell Osama!!! Pure Evil Hot Sauce, embellished with the following text: "Osama Bin Laden is truly the world's biggest Scumbag. He kills and then hides out in caves like the cowardly punk that he is. Prepare to meet your maker *loser*! You have assured yourself a cozy little spot in *Hell*! Hope you enjoy the ride!" Enough said.

Your political ire and rage at the state of the world spent, you may want to shift your focus back to pleasure. After all, life is short. Slip the Red Hot Chile Peppers' *Californication* into the sound system, let your erotic imagination run free, and sample some hot sauce. Its aphrodisiac properties, not to mention those provocative labels, will make life seem worth living once again.

Conclusion

A Short Meditation on Hellfire and Damnation

*Ye serpent, ye generation of vipers,
how can ye escape the damnation of hell?*
OUR LORD JESUS CHRIST, IN MATTHEW 23:33

Humble God-fearing chilehead that I am, I would never consider myself a member of that "generation of vipers." Yet Vicious Viper Hot Sauce is three times hotter than hell, and a bottle of it is lying dormant in my fridge (for the moment). And I have a friend who is Southern Baptist born-again, a real babe and a hot-sauce fanatic to boot—is she going to hell in a handbasket too? She can't be. I can't be. While it's true that when we partake of a truly hot hot sauce, we take one step closer to the aforementioned damnation—but, thank Christ, it's only a transient closeness.

This biblical voyage in and around hot sauce had its beginnings in my tender youth, and I suspect that it will not end until the day I die. I could suggest, tongue-in-cheek, that the hottest sauce in my collection could help that day arrive much sooner, but that would undermine my own attempts to inform the novice chileheads among you of the chile pepper's wonderful health benefits.

We now know that the belief that hot sauce causes ulcers is an old wives' tale. Indeed, it turns out that the opposite might be true. Certainly, people whose national cuisines are drenched with the sauce will attest to the curative power of chiles. We also know that capsaicin—the source of a pepper's heat and the incandescent culinary protagonist of this little book—improves the digestive system by stimulating stomach secretions. And we know that red-hot chile peppers have a laxative effect; they trigger the release of endorphins; they help stave off the common cold by irritating mucous membranes; and they can reduce high blood pressure. They may even protect us from some forms of cancer. Well, I believe it. Don't you?

Elsewhere, I spoke quite frankly about the chile's value as an aphrodisiac. Some also maintain that it increases the metabolic rate, thereby causing the body to burn more calories. So, sprinkle some habañero flakes on your pasta or pizza or salad, and maybe you'll shed a couple of pounds. Sadly, I can't claim that this has worked for me, but give it a try anyway. Who knows what can happen? Call it an experiment in extreme dieting.

These are all good things. But what about hot sauce's dark side? Why does hell figure prominently in so much hot-sauce advertising and in the rhetoric of the converted? In the Old Testament and the New, hell is a furnace of unquenchable fire, a place of everlasting punishment where sinners are tormented in both their bodies and their minds without surcease. You don't want to go there. Or do you?

Hot-sauce hell is a domain stripped of God's infinite mercy wherein God's wrath is revealed as an all-consuming, unforgiving fire. Those consigned to it are made to suffer in perpetuity. John the Baptist spoke of hell's "unquenchable fire," and Revelation refers to hell as "a lake of fire burning with brimstone." Can you even imagine the sheer torment these ancient words describe? In your effort to imagine, my fellow chileheads, contemplate your past experience with Dave's Special Reserve, or Pure Cap, or any other diabolically hot "food additive." Recall how every part of your body was consumed by the conflagration, how every iota of your being writhed in torment. And how long could you stand it? In perpetuity?

So, hellfire equals capsaicin. That good old mountain dew, colorless and innocuous-looking upon first inspection, can be as brutal as ignited napalm in the mouth. Or as brutal as scalding water on the genitalia, should you make the dire mistake of relieving yourself after handling a hot pepper and neglecting to wash your hands. (Chile-handling certainly serves to improve one's personal hygiene. Forget just once to wash your hands well before and after using the facilities, and the lesson will be permanently seared on your memory. You can take my word for it.)

Yes, Mr. Chilehead avers that hot-sauce hell is a very real place. (The hot-sauce void is also pretty hellish, as any chilehead who drains his or her last bottle after the market has closed will tell you. Cold turkey is purgatory, to be avoided at all costs. Addicted chileheads must vigilantly monitor their inventories. But I digress.) Hot-sauce hell may be found in the exotic nether regions of the culinary map, its expanse marked by telling symbols —skull and crossbones, tiny dentist's chairs and drills, tarantulas, scorpions, vampires, glowing chile peppers. Welcome to Painland.

Hot-sauce hell is a domain of fire and brimstone, a place of everlasting fire. Hear, my flock, these words of Jesus Christ: "So it shall be at the end of the world: the angels shall come forth, and sever the wicked from among the just, and shall cast them into the furnace of fire: there shall be wailing and gnashing of teeth" (Matthew 13:49–50). Well, I have ingested too much Habanero 750 and wailed piteously; I have served myself a generous portion of Satan's Blood and gnashed my teeth in agony. The liquid flames that rained down from heaven upon Sodom and Gomorrah in the old days now flow from the sauce bottle onto the tip of the chilehead's tongue. They race to the roof of the mouth and course down the throat, singeing the vocal cords, and then they wage their assault on the helpless sphincter. In short, they transport you to hell. Fire and brimstone in a bottle shall burn the innocent and the wicked alike.

There's the conundrum. Why do we chileheads, as we burn in earthly hell, remain convinced that we've simultaneously been transported to the Elysian Fields, where only the virtuous are permitted to spend eternity basking in pleasure? Are we all masochists? Martyrs? Fools? Why do we seek Tartarus in a bottle, or in the eviscerated body of a habañero? Throughout this slender volume, I have tried to shed some light on this conundrum, with its rich ontological dimensions. Perhaps the puzzle is ultimately unsolvable. It's certainly difficult to put down, so before I leave you, let's explore it a little further.

"How art thou fallen from heaven, O Lucifer, son of the morning . . . thou hast said in thine heart, I will ascend into heaven, I will exalt my throne above the stars of God . . . Yet thou shalt be brought to hell, to the sides of the pit" (Isaiah 14:12–13, 15). We know that the conflict upon which this passage is built flourishes inside a hot-sauce bottle as well. We chileheads willingly enter hell with the expectation of heaven, we step unflinchingly into the fire in pursuit of fearsome pleasure. And as we engage in this paradoxical pursuit, experimenting with hotter and hotter sauces, the religious aspect of our obsession becomes apparent in another way. For diehard chileheads, sauce extremism powerfully evokes memories of Sunday School scripture classes and Bible-thumping preachers. The sauce leads us back in time through childhood rec- ollections such as these, and it compels us forward in time to the day we achieve the ultimate burn—the chilehead's state of grace.

We've reached the end of our journey, and your guide—Mr. Chilehead—will now take a well-deserved respite. I hope that by now you have all come to understand that we chileheads descend into an inferno closely resembling biblical hellfire because we know in our hearts that such a leap of faith will allow us access to the express elevator to culinary heaven. And on that upbeat note, my dear fellow chileheads, I lay down my pen. I have an elevator to catch and a hot date with The Grim Reaper (the sauce, that is).

Appendix 1
The Chile Pepper Institute

There is a place that is sacred to all chileheads, and it's right here on Earth. It's located in the heart of Painland. I refer to the acclaimed Chile Pepper Institute. All of us chileheads are happy and proud to have such a pilgrimage site—a center that practices sound scholarship and reveres the chile pepper. The following statement derives from the institute's Web site. Take heed of its message and, if the spirit moves you, sign up and join the converted.

> The Chile Pepper Institute is an international nonprofit organization devoted to education, research, publication, and archiving information related to Capsicums or chile peppers. The Institute also seeks to preserve chile germplasm, of both cultivated and wild species, and to further the studies of Capsicum diseases. Further, the Institute seeks to be an authoritative source of all types of information regarding Capsicum. It is a recognized University institute, organized and supported under the College of Agriculture and Home Economics of New Mexico State University.
>
> The primary programs and activities are: education through our ever-expanding, up-to-date World

Wide Web site; publication of the *Chile Pepper Institute Newsletter* and books on Capsicum-related subjects; research on new Capsicum cultivars and diseases; sponsoring and hosting the annual scholarly New Mexico Chile Conference.

The Institute also serves as a bank for chile germplasm and functions as an international clearinghouse and archive for information related to Capsicums. Currently we have a multifunctional kiosk display with "The Story of Chiles" at the New Mexico Farm and Ranch Heritage Museum in Las Cruces, NM. Included here is a solid oak display case, sponsored by members, that houses our "Hall of Flame" chile-decorated tiles . . . We also provide tours of our annual Teaching & Demonstration Garden with over 100 different varieties of chiles (www.chilepepperinstitute.org/Mission.htm).

Chileheads, potential chileheads, and other interested parties are invited to become members of the institute. New members receive a one-year subscription to the newsletter, a Chile Pepper Institute decal, some seed packets, and several other chile items. Membership categories and rates are: non-commercial member, $25; supporting member, $50; professional member, $100; small business member, $300; industry member, $1,000; and corporate member, $5,000.

You can contact the Chile Pepper Institute at hotchile@nmsu.eduContrary. And tell them Mr. Chilehead sent you, okay?

Appendix 2

The Inexperienced Chile Taster

This appendix is comprised of notes written by an inexperienced chile taster from New Jersey on a visit to Texas. I first saw the notes on pyropepper.com, the Web site of PyroMan, aka G. Grant Lane, purveyor of the fieriest hot sauces known to humankind. With his kind permission, I reproduce them here.

This little narrative offers us a glimpse, albeit a vividly profane one, of what life is like for new arrivals in Painland. And after you've read it, you can perhaps appreciate why its author chooses to remain anonymous (we'll call him Frank).*

> Recently, I was lucky enough to be the ten-thousandth attendee at the Texas State Fair, and I was asked to be a judge at a chile cook-off—apparently, the original judge number 3 had called in sick at the last moment, and I happened to be standing there when the call came in. I was assured by the other two judges (native Texans) that it would be a fun event and a true taste of Texas hospitality. They also assured me that the chile wouldn't be all that spicy and I could have free beer during the tasting. So I accepted. Here are the scorecards from the event:

CHILE #1
Mike's Maniac Mobster Monster Chile

Judge 1: A little too heavy on the tomato.
Amusing kick.
Judge 2: Nice, smooth tomato flavor. Very mild.
Frank: Holy shit, what the hell is this stuff? You could remove paint with it. Took me two beers to put the flames out. Hope that's the worst one . . . these Texans are crazy.

CHILE #2
Arthur's Afterburner Chile

Judge 1: Smoky, with a hint of pork.
Slight jalapeño tang.
Judge 2: Exciting barbecue flavor. Needs more peppers to be taken seriously.
Frank: Keep this out of reach of children! I'm not sure what I'm supposed to taste besides pain. I had to wave off two people who wanted to give me the Heimlich maneuver. They had to walkie-talkie in three extra beers when they saw the look on my face.

CHILE #3
Fred's Famous Burn Down the Barn Chile

Judge 1: Excellent firehouse chile! Great kick.
Needs more beans.
Judge 2: A bit salty. Good use of red peppers.
Frank: Call the EPA, I've located a uranium spill! My nose feels like I've been snorting Drano. Every

one knows the routine by now. Barmaid pounded me on the back; now my backbone is in the front of my chest. I'm getting shit-faced.

CHILE #4
Bubba's Black Magic

Judge 1: Black bean chile with almost no spice. Disappointing.

Judge 2: Hint of lime in the black beans. Good side dish for fish or other mild foods; not much of a chile.

Frank: I felt something scraping across my tongue but was unable to taste it. Shelly, the barmaid, was standing behind me with refills; that 300-pound bitch is starting to look *hot*, just like this nuclear waste I'm eating.

CHILE #5
Linda's Legal Lip Remover

Judge 1: Meaty, strong chile. Cayenne peppers freshly ground, adding considerable kick.
Very impressive.

Judge 2: Chile using shredded beef; could use more tomato. Must admit that the cayenne peppers make a strong statement.

Frank: My ears are ringing, and I can no longer focus my eyes. I farted and four people behind me burst into flames. The contestant seemed offended when I told her that her chile had caused me brain damage. Shelly saved my tongue from bleeding by pouring beer directly on it from a pitcher. It really pisses me off that the other judges asked me to stop screaming. The heck with those rednecks!

CHILE #6
Vera's Very Vegetarian Variety

Judge 1: Thin, yet bold vegetarian-variety chile. Good balance of spice and peppers.

Judge 2: The best yet. Aggressive use of peppers, onions, and garlic. Superb.

Frank: My intestines are now a straight pipe filled with gaseous, sulfuric flames. No one seems inclined to stand behind me except that slut Shelly. I need to wipe my ass with a snow cone!

CHILE #7
Susan's Screaming Sensation Chile

Judge 1: A mediocre chile, over-reliant on canned peppers.

Judge 2: Ho hum—tastes as if the chef literally threw in a can of chile peppers at the last moment. I should note that I am worried about judge number 3. He appears distressed, and he's cursing uncontrollably.

Frank: You could put a grenade in my mouth, pull the pin, and I wouldn't feel a damn thing. I've lost the sight in one eye, and the world sounds like it's made of rushing water. My shirt is covered with chile that has dribbled out of my mouth. My pants are full of lava-like shit that matches my damn shirt. At least the people performing the autopsy will know right away what killed me. I've decided to stop breathing; it's too painful. If I need air, I'll just suck it in through the four-inch hole in my stomach.

CHILE #8
Helen's Mount Saint Chile

Judge 1: A perfect ending. This is a nice blended offering, safe for all, not too bold, but spicy enough to declare its existence.

Judge 2: This final entry is a good, balanced chile, neither mild nor hot. Sorry to see that most of it was lost when judge number 3 passed out, knocking the pot over on himself. Not sure if he's going to make it. Poor Yank.

Frank: [Editor's note: judge number 3 was unable to report.]

*pyropepper.com/docroot/cookoff.html

Appendix 3

Mirror, Mirror on the Wall, What Are Mr. Chilehead's Picks for the Hottest Sauces of Them All?

The Source
Certified at 7.1 million Scoville units! Thus far, the hottest thing in a bottle. You a dumb-ass wussy? Try this, and be cured right out of this life. Produced by Original Juan.

Blair's 5 a.m. Reserve
This 5.5-to-6-million-Scoville-unit super-collectible is from Blair Gardner, sauce savant and uncompromising maker of the Death Sauce product line.

Blair's 4 a.m. Reserve
This one's in the 4-million-plus Scoville range, and it sells for big bucks on eBay and the like.

Blair's 3 a.m. Reserve
In the 1.5-to-2-million Scoville range (Blair never specifies), 3 a.m. is one of PyroMan's all-time best-selling products.

Da' Bomb: The Final Answer
From Original Juan and tested by an outside laboratory, this sauce is 1.5 million Scoville units of pure heat. Pyro-Man classifies it as the world's hottest actual hot sauce (as opposed to extract), and Mr. Chilehead agrees.

Smack My Ass and Call Me Sally: Chet's Gone Mad
Another 1.5-million-Scoville sauce. Produced for Brian Wheeler's Tijuana Flats Burrito Company of Orlando, Florida.

Pyro Diablo
A single drop of this wicked, 1.5-million-Scoville-unit concoction will push the temperature of any dish into the red sector. Best used with extreme caution; the eyedropper in the cap discourages foolhardiness.

Gold Cap
Made with imported African capsicum extract and weighing in at 1 million Scovilles, Gold Cap is remarkable in that it has no chemical flavor. Reputedly used in minute quantities by several renowned New Orleans chefs to lend an authentic flavor to regional specialties. Comes handily packaged with its own working fire extinguisher. (Don't giggle, you might need it!)

Mad Dog's Revenge
This killer extract—at 1 million Scovilles—comes from "Mad Dog" David Ashley of Boston's Ashley Foods.

Ashley also produces the legendary Mad Dog Inferno hot sauce. Revenge is PyroMan's best-selling extract.

Cool Million Extract
From the Poison Pepper Company of St. Petersburg, Florida, and manufactured by the good folks at Sauce Crafters, this one's certified 1 million Scovilles; great collectible packaging.

Blair's 2 a.m. Reserve
The original Blair's a.m. rates 900,000 Scovilles.

Satan's Blood
A super-collectible from Sauce Crafters that boasts 800,000 Scoville units.

Unbearable
A 750,000-Scoville-unit collectible in an innocuously cute bear-shaped bottle. It's made by Jim Campbell (no relation to Mr. Chilehead), an Indianapolis fireman whose WildPepper company is one of the few certified growers of the legendary red savina habañero.

Smack My Ass and Call Me Sally: The Slap Heard Around the World
A 700,000-Scoville killer from Tijuana Flats.

Blair's Mega Death
A 550,000-Scoville-unit hot sauce from the masterful Blair.

Pure Cap
Weighing in at 500,000 Scovilles, this was the first extract to hit the market. It comes in a pill bottle armed with an eyedropper, and it's manufactured for Garden Row Foods, a hot-sauce distributor.

Hard Time
At 400,000 Scoville units, this is the hottest product from "CaJohn" Hard, a fire-protection engineer and owner of CaJohn's Fiery Foods. An oleoresin of capsaicin measuring 2 million Scovilles blended with red savina habañeros makes this one of the most incendiary sauces sold today. Hard times a-comin', indeed, if you go overboard with this stuff.

357 Mad Dog
A 357,000-Scoville sauce from "Mad Dog" David Ashley.

Dave's Private Reserve
The hottest of the hot from the godfather of demonic extracts Dave Hirschkopf of Dave's Gourmet. It rates 300,000 Scovilles, and it's a perennial collector's item.

Possible Side Effects
Produced for the famous comedy troupe of the same name by Blair himself; 283,000 Scoville units.

Vicious Viper
A German company makes this 250,000-Scoville-unit elixir for Suncoast Peppers.

Appendix 4

Wilbur Scoville's Painland Scale

The magic oil that fires the chile is called capsaicin. This potent substance is immanent in the veins of the fruit (not the seeds, as some believe), and it enflames the nerve endings in the mouth and throat. Indeed, it is so hellish hot that if you were to dilute one part in 100,000 parts of water and have a tiny sip, then your tongue would blister. Capsaicin's heat, as you by now well know, is measured in Scoville units.

This system of heat measurement was invented in 1912 by pharmacologist Wilbur Scoville. He assembled a panel of five taste testers to enact the procedure. These brave individuals first ascertained the exact weight of a chile pepper; next, they extracted the chile's capsaicin and dissolved it in alcohol; then they diluted the solution with sugar water until it could no longer be discerned by the palate. When they had completed these steps, it was time to taste the pain — I mean heat. The tasters would keep adjusting the dilution until they could detect the heat. Thus, if the dilution was 1,000 parts water to 1 part capsaicin solution, then the chile under examination would be assigned a Scoville rating of 1,000 units. Three out of five tasters had to agree before the rating was established. Of course, this method was highly subjective.

Nowadays, human tasters are eschewed in favor of a process called high performance liquid chromatography, or HPLC. This process measures capsaicin in parts per million, and the results are converted to Scoville units. HPLC has thus put a cap on the taste of pain for Wilbur Scoville's teams of fearless pioneer tasters, who singed their tongues in the interests of science.

The pepper that incarnates the pure taste of pain is my beloved habañero. It holds an unassailable position at the top of the Scoville scale, outstripped only by pure capsaicin. Let's see how some of our favorite chiles rate on the Scoville scale and allow ourselves to imagine the heavenly/hellish heat.

Pure capsaicin: 16 million units (Toto! We are no longer in Kansas!)
Red savina habañero: 350,000–550,000 units
Habañero and Scotch bonnet: 100,000–500,000 units
Thai and chiltepin: 70,000–80,000 units
Santaka: 50,000–60,000 units
Tabasco: 30,000–50,000 units
Cayenne: 35,000–40,000 units
Chilipiquin: 30,000–40,000 units
Chile de árbol: 15,000–30,000 units
Serrano: 7,000–25,000 units
Jalapeño: 3,500–4,500 units
Ancho poblano: 2,500–3,000 units
Anaheim: 1,000–1,500 units
Bell pepper: 0 units (We return to Kansas.)

Appendix 5
You Know You're a Chilehead If . . .

On his Mark's ReMarkable Web site, chilehead Mark Stevens includes the following list, which should make all good chileheads chuckle and non-chileheads scratch their heads. It is reproduced here, in an abridged and modified version, with Mark's kind permission.* So, without further ado,

You Know You're a Chilehead If:

- You don't have to worry about your roommates stealing your food.
- Your toilet paper spontaneously combusts after use.
- Dave Hirschkopf thinks *you're* crazy.
- Your chile recipe is in violation of more than one nuclear weapons proliferation treaty.
- Your used Kleenex tissues glow in the dark.
- Nobody asks you to do the cooking at your family reunion.
- Your kitchen utensils were designed and built by NASA.
- You're tired of people asking about those dried Thai peppers floating around in your breakfast cereal.
- Your pepper garden is visible from the moon.

- You use capsaicin-based pain ointment as a food additive.
- You have to file an environmental-impact statement every time you make a batch of salsa.
- The diaper service refuses to pick up your baby's soiled diapers.
- You go to a medical clinic for a routine blood test and you get the strangest looks.
- You go to a medical clinic for a routine blood test and you get the strangest looks and your name isn't DancesWithCarp.
- You know every single one of Scott Sehlhorst's middle names.
- More than half the souvenirs from your last tropical vacation were hot sauces and spices.
- For your monthly Mo Hotta Mo Betta order you get free shipping and handling.
- You throw a scrap of food to the dog and he looks at you as if to say, "You must think I'm an idiot!"
- All reading material in your house contains at least one of the following words in the title: "Chile," "MO," "Pepper," "Hot."
- You've seen jicama/vidalia one time too many.
- You can correctly spell and pronounce "chipotle" and "capsicum," and you know to which food group they belong.
- You never go into a food store without checking the selection and prices of hot peppers and hot sauces.

- Your refrigerator door has more than 30 bottles of hot sauce stored in it.
- The sissy salsa you made accidentally set most of your guests on fire.
- You have at least one item of clothing or a coffee mug emblazoned with chiles.
- The law requires you to build a six-foot-high fence around your swimming pool and chile garden.
- Your flatulence is capable of peeling the paint off the walls.
- Your hands are so tough from handling hot peppers that you occasionally forget and touch something that isn't so tough.
- "Hotluck" is a word in your vocabulary, and you've been to one.
- "Ring of fire" and "burns twice" actually mean something to you.
- You suspect that botulism can't grow in the habañero-based sauce you created last winter, and you aren't afraid to test the theory—on your brother-in-law.
- You take your own bottle of Inner Beauty Sauce to restaurants.
- You have more that three kinds of Inner Beauty Sauce in your fridge.
- You can tell the difference between the "original" and the "new" Inner Beauty sauces.
- You consider chips to be only a means of carrying salsa from the bowl to your mouth.

- You rate chile by how long it takes to make the skin under your eyes sweat.
- You rate all foods by how long they take to make your nose run.
- You apply capsaicin in unorthodox ways; for example, you snort powdered peppers like snuff.
- You don't know how hot a salsa really is until you kiss someone and he or she runs for the nearest faucet.
- You know more about TMV, botulism, and white flies than the staff of your local county extension office.
- You know what a "tilde" is and how to use it.
- You have a bottle of contact-lens-wetting solution in your kitchen, and you know how to use it.
- You have put chile peppers into your smoker—by themselves.
- You've danced with carp, howled for habañeros, sought chile sisters, taped a cat, or jerked a chicken.
- You are frequently described by a name composed of the words "leather" or "asbestos" followed by the words "mouth," "ass," or "butt."
- You have more than one molcajete not in use as a speaker stand.
- You know how to make horseradish and why you shouldn't.
- You hand out ripe habañeros to trick-or-treaters when you run out of candy, but first you draw little jack o' lantern faces on them—"They're itty bitty pumpkins!"

ADVENTURES IN THE TASTE OF PAIN 167

- People laugh when you invite them over for dinner, look at you like you're crazy, and walk away without answering.
- People suddenly remember that the very night you've invited them for dinner, they'll be having that elective surgery they've been postponing for years. (And they actually have the surgery instead of coming for dinner, figuring, correctly, that it'll hurt less.)
- You laugh (devilishly) when you invite newbies for dinner.
- It's not mealtime, it's time for a fix.
- You accidentally add a glop instead of a drop of that radioactive hot sauce (the one with the chemical taste and smell) and say to yourself, "Oh well, it can't be *that* hot"—and it isn't.
- You have mornings when you can't tell if your butt is sweating or crying.
- Your friends try to find something too hot for you —and fail.
- Your friends ask if you're going to put hot sauce on your pumpkin pie—and you do.
- You label temporary computer backup files "*.hab."
- After five years, your sister still complains that your chile ruined her stomach.
- The waitress doesn't believe you when you order.
- You own stock in Tucks, the medicated-pad company.
- You've eaten salsa, with the words "Insanity" or "Hell" in the name, straight.

- You're a bachelor or college student, and the following things can be said about you: you can make a Taco Bell burrito taste good; you think that a hot date involves just you, a chile pot, and a dozen habañeros; you drink chile beer from a bong; the word "capsicum" turns you on; you know what "sexually transmitted capsaicin" means.
- You've tried to smoke a jalapeño.
- You mix habs into the cheese before stuffing your poppers, for flavor.
- You've seen jicama/vidalia one time too many.
- You know what a "merkin" is—in both Texan and English.
- You consider eating hornworms because the capsaicin in them may not be digested.
- You keep—at the very least—salsa, sauce, and dried ground peppers in your desk drawer for booster shots to get you through the workday.
- You brag about the size of your pepper(s).
- You use cheap beer for three things: drinking, making chile, and killing slugs.
- You get excited when someone says, "They don't make it hot enough!"
- You believe that if it doesn't quicken your pulse, it ain't worth eating.
- You know enough about substance P to talk to a premed at a cocktail party.
- You remember Curtis "A Recipe for Every Occasion" Jackson.

- You have a collection of chile .gifs and .jpegs.
- You've seen jicama/vidalia one time too many.
- You enjoy watching big-ego-idiots (one word) gulp water like lizards.
- You screen dates by ordering poppers or skins as appetizers.
- You dance the chilehead cha-cha.
- You have a paintbrush and use it for sexual purposes.
- You have disdain for NH cops, and you donated to the cook's legal defense fund.
- You load your air rifle with tiny chile peppers when hunting the neighbor's cat.
- You've seen jicama/vidalia one time too many.
- You toss the evening's ration of chiles into the wok and the ensuing blast of vapor sends everyone running from the kitchen crying and coughing.
- You have passed out from the fumes while cooking your favorite dish.
- Your friends have passed out from the fumes while you were cooking your favorite dish.
- You have passed out while eating your favorite dish.
- You have a World War II surplus gas mask in your kitchen and you use it while cooking.
- You get your family to leave the house when you make your version of General Tsao's chicken.
- You have had to sit on an inner tube for three days because your salsa was too hot.

- Your significant other has offered you a Popsicle while you were in the bathroom.
- You have asked your significant other to get you a Popsicle while you were in the bathroom.
- You sometimes have fingertip indentations in your thighs when you exit the bathroom.
- Your children can eat hotter food than you can.
- You've seen jicama/vidalia one time too many.
- You have told a restaurant hostess that you're there for the chilehead gathering.
- Your regular waiter automatically brings you IB, Melinda's, El Eyucatao, and takes the water glasses away.
- You've often sent food back because it was not hot enough.
- You have sent or received contraband chile seeds from a foreign country.
- You keep spare rolls of toilet tissue in the freezer.
- Your shorts have strange bleach marks on them, even though you never use bleach.
- Your flatulence has a whole codicil of its own in the Geneva Convention on Chemical and Biological Warfare.
- People would rather eat with Margaret Thatcher than with you.
- People are always coming up to you and saying, "Here, try this one."
- You name your pepper plants.
- People all over the world know the names of your pepper plants.

- You think of Tabasco in the same way you think of salt.
- You use Tabasco instead of Binaca.
- You have most of Dave DeWitt's books.
- You can debate the advantages and disadvantages of putting batch numbers on Inner Beauty Real Hot Sauce.
- You've gone to Bourbon Street in Burlington and called the chef a wimp.
- People will challenge you to hot-food-eating competitions—once.
- When cooking, you often start sneezing.
- Cutting onions does not make you cry.
- People know not to borrow your "hand" cream, and friends are afraid to shake your hand when they meet you.
- Your favorite way to eat a taco is to use a different type of hot sauce or salsa with every bite.
- You freezer is filled with chiles and chile powder; your refrigerator is filled with pickled chiles, hot sauces, salsas, and chile beer; your cabinets are filled with canned or bottled chiles and chile products. And you still wonder if you have enough chiles to get you through the winter.
- You consider any source of fresh peppers within a two-hour drive local.
- You yell "Jicama! Vidalia!" at rude drivers.
- You shop at stores where you can't speak the language and still come out with at least three new hot sauces or hot pastes or hot foods.

- At Thai/Szechwan/Korean restaurants the waiters stop to watch you eat.
- Your favorite restaurant takes the 911 pasta off the menu, but the chef will make up a special batch just for you.
- You hear your waiter yell to the cook, "Make it *hot*! It's for that crazy chilehead!"
- You know all about the dangers of using your pepper grinder to grind anything other than chiles, but you still do it—and you *love* it!
- You pay your local nursery to take care of your pepper plants when you go on a trip—or you take them with you.
- Your friends ask you to make them some of your special sauce and then use it to clean their silverware.
- Your fingerprints instantly tarnish your own silverware.
- Your bottled sauces explode and you don't clean the splatters off the walls and ceiling because they make good conversation pieces.
- You kiss your girlfriend/boyfriend/spouse/pleasant stranger, and they say the chiles you just ate are hurting them.
- You use more propane than the plumber next door.
- You know what "ch" means.
- Your breath can set off the smoke detector.
- Your breath can *melt* the smoke detector.
- You leave scorch marks on the pillow.
- You leave scorch marks on the sheets.

- You recite pH levels to go to sleep.
- Your supermarket labels all peppers as either "hot" or "sweet," and it bothers you.
- You tell the produce manager the proper pepper names.
- The toilet water starts boiling when you go to the bathroom.
- You know why you're supposed to wash your hands *before* you go to the bathroom.
- Your office mates get nervous when you exit the restroom smiling, with tears running down your face.
- Indoor pests are no longer flies, but aphids.
- You use cayenne instead of Vick's VapoRub to relieve your kids' congestion.
- The wallpaper in your house is peeling, and there's no humidity.
- Your local tool-rental center wants to rent you out as a paint stripper.
- Your heating bill has dropped 30 percent for no apparent reason.
- You add the category "Spicy" to your MCII cookbook software, and all your recipes fit into that category.
- You fling aside the Victoria's Secret catalog to get to the chilehead mail-order catalogs.
- Your family members actually steal the hot sauces out of your fridge because you have the best and they don't know where you got them.

- You deplete your hot stash at work and have to raid the condiment area of the cafeteria for crushed red pepper and Tabasco just to survive the day.
- You arrive at work to find between 50 and 100 e-mail messages waiting for you, most of them chile-related.
- You seriously think about replacing your regular Christmas lights with chile lights and leaving them up all year long.
- You regard terms like "very hot" and "hot" on manufactured products with great skepticism.
- Certain stores call you when a new hot product comes in.
- You've considered opening a chile store so you could have a constant supply.
- You live in a large city, but every store that sells something hot knows your name and your telephone number.
- You take out crop insurance on three jalapeños, four habañeros, and a poblano—again.
- When a severe hailstorm threatens, you act to protect the car, the dog, and the chile plants, not necessarily in that order.
- You value your pepper patch so highly that you try to talk your bank into giving you a pepper equity loan. You get a chilly reception.
- You change your will and establish a fund to provide a chile reservation for your cherished plants.
- You try to market a game called "Chipotle," in which players answer questions relating to chile

ADVENTURES IN THE TASTE OF PAIN 175

lore. "Double Chipotle" brings down a lawsuit.
- You soak your dental floss in Tabasco.
- The condensed layer on your kitchen walls could be used as a condiment.
- You not only know the IUPAC names of the capsaicinoids, but you can also draw the structures and are working on synthetic methods based on common household chemicals.
- You measure the heat of your peppers by HPLC and send the best specimens out for GC-MS analysis.
- You know that gustatory cells don't sweat.
- You are trying to graft different peppers onto one plant with phased flowering to avoid cross-pollination.
- You overhear your children telling each other nursery stories—". . . and when she opened the door she saw three steaming bowls of chile on the table . . ."—and you smile.
- You love Thai food so much that "prik" becomes part of your social vocabulary, with unfortunate consequences.
- You watch *Voyager*, and you could swear the First Officer's name is "Chipotle."
- You get stuck in a blizzard in the middle of nowhere, but you don't care because you're carrying . . . a bottle of hot sauce.
- You stop eating lunch with work friends who won't eat spicy food; you create a new lunch bunch with nothing more in common than a willingness to visit

every ethnic restaurant in the area in search of spicy food.
- You consider the taste of chiles coming up as well as going down.
- You know what "Hunan hand" is but still refuse to wear gloves.
- Despite being a skiing/snowboarding fiend, you're still glad for a very warm, sunny November because it's good for the pepper crop.
- You live in a chile-scarce region, and when friends visit from chile-abundant areas you make them bring you chiles in exchange for room and board.
- You not only wait impatiently for the mailman to bring you your official chilehead card, but you also go to the post office to make sure they haven't misplaced it or anything.
- You know how to aid in the conception of chiles by using a vibrator.
- You consider habañeros to be one the four basic food groups.
- You know why DancesWithCarp's brother gives raccoons late-night bicycle rides.
- You've actually read this list to this point.
- You know what Mac Geek eats for lunch, and it does not scare you.
- You've experimented with bacon, cinnamon, maple syrup, and habs for breakfast.
- You've devised ingenious and horrific ways of terminating slugs in your chile garden; the faster they dissolve, the better!

- You dare not touch the rubber gasket in your blender.
- You believe that if you can still see the waitress, then you haven't had enough pepper.
- You drink hot sauce straight from the bottle, because who needs anything to put it on?
- You can argue about how to make traditional guacamole like a Texan argues about making chile.
- The police check out your backyard because your neighbors see you out there at night with a flashlight working on your garden and think you're growing pot because they can't identify your plants —and besides, who gardens at night?
- Members of the DEA knock at your door because you've ordered grow lights.
- You think that crop rotation means pulling up the orange habs and replacing them with red savina habs.
- You can levitate without practicing TM.
- You can sweat without exercising.
- All the cats in your neighborhood are bald.
- You grow chiles in the bathroom, the spare bedroom, the kitchen, the front garden, the back garden, and in the hanging basket by the front door.
- Your local photo-shop manager no longer stares at you when you collect the close-ups of your chile plants.
- You choose your dinner to go with the hot sauce you've selected.

- You buy a house just because it has a pepper garden in the back.
- You add habañero powder to five-alarm chile without tasting it first.
- You have dessert recipes that call for habañeros.
- You sprinkle habañero powder on your vanilla yogurt, and when it fails to burn enough ...
- You swish your food around in your mouth to spread the burn.
- Your head explodes and your whole body goes up in flames, and even your urine burns.
- You always save some of the hot chile/garlic sauce when eating in a Chinese restaurant to go with the sorbet dessert.
- You pull the plastic stopper out of a bottle of Melinda's XXX because it makes the sauce come out too slowly, then you suck all the good stuff out.
- You start to follow horses around carrying a bucket and a spade, a glint in your eye.
- You've seen jicama/vidalia one time too many.
- You tried Jim's Red Savina Bread even after hearing the shrieks and moans of those who tried it before you.
- Your name is on the chilehead homepage member list.
- You got a hug from FireGirl!
- You have a vague idea what "schmuckendrops" is/are.
- You plan to retire in New Mexico.
- You actually rent—and watch—a really bad movie

like *Dumb and Dumber* just because you read somewhere that it contained a scene involving hot sauce or hot peppers.
- You know what "shrimping" is and would consider trying it with salsa.
- You risk "Hunan eye" by trying to pour every last speck of the Ass Kickin' Habanero Peanuts into your mouth.
- Your girlfriend doses your Negra Modelo with El Yucateco and you don't notice—except that the flavor improves!
- You enjoy a good case of anodynia in the morning.
- You instinctively rub your eyes with your wrist or the back of your hand because you've developed a permanent capsaicin residue on your fingertips.
- You dilute your Dave's Insanity with Tabasco.
- You dilute your Tabasco with Dave's Insanity.
- You consider using diluted hot-sauce spray to keep your cats from eating your *dracaena marginata*.
- You run out of Calvin's Chile Powder before you run out of things to put it on.
- You did not squirm and cross your legs when you read about the incontinent having capsaicin injected by catheter into their overactive bladders.
- You object to objections about someone objecting to ads for Tabasco Jeeps.
- To get to a chilehead dinner you are willing to ride in the back of a Chevy Suburban and risk being crushed by shifting crates containing 75 pounds of chipotles.

- You use a complimentary round-trip airline ticket to get to the Fiery Food Show in Albuquerque.
- McD's new ad for a Mucho Macho McBurger with McSalsa catches your attention as you walk past the TV, and, screaming, you vow to triple the size of your chile plot next year.
- You've been through at least three "Why not set up a chilehead newsgroup?" debates.
- You've seen jicama/vidalia one time too many.
- You become deliriously happy when you find adult lacewings lurking among your chile plants.
- You have engaged in knock-down-and-drag-out flame wars over the ingredients in your bug spray.
- You engage in serious discussions about what type of pee works best to repel critters from your chile patch.
- You have the equivalent of a master's degree in botulin growing conditions.
- You sought grief counseling after hearing of the problems with the 1999 Hatch chile crop.
- You can recite the timeline of ownership of *Chile Pepper Magazine* from memory.
- You are willing to admit that you mistook double-strength capsaicin pain-paste for a jock-itch remedy and go into some detail about the repercussions.
- You have a computer in the kitchen and suffer from "Hunan keyboard."
- Raccoons knock over all the trashcans on your street but leave yours alone.

- You throw soaked hab powder onto the sauna oven.
- You make your favorite habañero-based sauce, wash your hands twice, and make a grocery list; two days later, your wife, pen sucker extraordinaire, starts screaming, "What did you do to my f——pen?!?!"
- You buy a second refrigerator to hold your sauce bottles so you can fit in a turkey for the family at Christmas.
- You make gravlax (Swedish salted salmon) with habañero powder.
- Your starting instructions for pepper seeds are:
  1. Fill starting trays with soil, add seeds, add water
  2. Look for signs of growth
  3. Put tray in warm location
  4. Look for signs of growth
  5. Make dinner
  6. Return to seed tray; look for signs of growth
  7. Repeat step 6 every 10 minutes for approximately 10 days
  8. Jump for joy at first sign of growth
  9. Post news of first sign of growth to chilehead list
  10. Return to tray to make sure plants are still growing
  11. Repeat step 10
  12. Repeat step 11
- You know what the "burnt cat hair" effect is.
- Every time you vacuum, you find at least one pepper seed in the dust bag; you are so obsessed

with pepper seeds that you actually search your dust bag for them.
- You've seen jicama/vidalia one time too many.
- You can remember the nutrients and values of the composted cow flop you use for your pepper plants better than your children's birthdays.
- You actually request mail containing dangerous powders.
- You braid chiles into your hair for the holidays.
- You wake up every morning speaking like Cartman.
- You add Pure Cap to your toothpaste in order to remove plaque.
- You can travel the world and ask for peppers in any language even though you don't know how to order a meal.
- You get a chile-pepper tattoo.
- You make a prosthetic nipple from a plastic glove and fill it with habañero sauce.

*www.exit109.com/~mstevens/ykyaci.html

Appendix 6

Mr. Chilehead's Web Sites That Matter

The Internet has become a critical resource for chileheads. There is, in fact, an overabundance of chile information in cyberspace, and navigating your way through it can be pretty daunting. Over time, I have compiled a list of the more interesting sites, and to aid you in your spicy adventures, I'll share that list with you.

But before I present my full list, I want to make a few special recommendations. First, I believe that one of the best sites on the Web is pyropepper.com, which is run by my dear friend and fellow chilehead G. Grant Lane, aka PyroMan. Here are PyroMan's musings on the state of the heat: "I believe that our industry is in its infancy. As awareness of the health benefits, novelty, and plain *fun* of chile-related products continues to permeate the mainstream, I expect an explosion of the fiery culture heretofore unimaginable. Fascination with fire dates back to our advent upon the earth . . . It touches something deep within us all and warms our hearts (and everything else!). I believe that the chile pepper represents the primordial fire from whence we all sprang forth." PyroMan's site is very user-friendly; it features a helpful grouping of items from the hottest to the not so hot. And PyroMan packages his wares carefully—a crucial service for chileheads like Mr. Chilehead, who has suffered many broken bottles in the post.

I must also make mention of Dave's Gourmet site, at www.davesgourmet.com. I, for one, could not live without the fire that roars inside Dave's specialty items. And then there's the extraordinary Blair, with his irreproachable death sauces. Check out www.eXtremefood.com if you know what's good for you. You can download Blair's complete print catalog from the site.

A most invaluable site on the Web is fieryfoods.com, Dave DeWitt's extravagant homage to the chile pepper and a profound resource for chileheads. Everything you wanted to know but were afraid to ask about chiles can be found there.

Many of my favorite sites are members of The Ring of Fire, the most comprehensive Web index extant of hot-and-spicy-food-related Web pages. It is a continuous loop of sites equipped with Next and Previous buttons that take you from one site to the next within the linked community. Very ergonomic. In its founders' words, the ring is devoted to "the enjoyment of cooking and eating hot and spicy foods and growing and worshiping chile peppers."

Gardeners take note: At the end of my list of Web sites that matter, I've included a separate list of sites that dispense chile-pepper seeds. Here, then, is my list of the sites that matter most, followed by a list of sites that are well worth a visit. They all enrich the chilehead's existence.

WEB SITES THAT MATTER MOST

National Hot Pepper Association
400 N.W. 20th Street
Fort Lauderdale, FL 33311-3818
(954) 565-4972
www.inter-linked.com/org/nhpa/
This trade association publishes a quarterly 28-page newsletter; membership is $20 a year.

Chileheads Online
www.chileheadsonline.com
The name says it all—it's the chilehead place to be.

U.K. Chile-Head
easyweb.easynet.co.uk/~gcaselton/chile/chile.html
Brit chilehead Graeme Caselton's super-informative site.

The Fiery Foods Supersite
www.fiery-foods.com
The domain of the Pope of Peppers.

Pepperworld
www.pepperworld.com
The German locale for all things hot; check out the hot shop.

FireGirl.com
www.firegirl.com
The gals at FireGirl.com have an extravagantly tasty site with many rare and incendiary products on offer.

Other Sites That Matter

Since Web addresses change so frequently, I have not included them here; so use a good search engine to get you where you're going.

Armadillo Crossing
Arturo's Maui Onion Salsa
Bachri's Chili & Spice Gourmet (sauces and spices from Indonesia, and Bachri's own Sambal Tumis hot sauce)
Bandana Bandito (Tex-Mex sauces and salsas)
Bandana's (all-natural hot-pepper products, jalapeño ketchup)
Big Daddy's General Store (spice mixes, cookbooks, all the fixins)
Biosphere Chile Page
Black Sage's Sauces
Blazing Chile Brothers (hot salsas, hot sauces)
Blue Armadillo
Bob's Fiery Foods (hot sauces, salsas, chile, hot nuts, snacks)
Boo-Daddy's Chile Pepper Company
Brown Adobe (salsas, hot sauces)
CaJohn's Fiery Foods
California Sunshine Foods
Capt'n Sleepy's Habanero
Chesapeake Heat (hot sauces, fresh and dried peppers)
Chile Connection

Chile Stop

Chile Today (Hot Tamale Hot Sauce of the Month Club)

Chilegod (searchable hot-sauce database)

Chilehead Central (you gotta go there!)

ChileHead (chile-pepper discussion list)

Chili Bob Products (hot chile mixes)

Chili New Mexico's Finest

Chili Ristras (handmade gifts)

Chiliman Hot Gifts

Chilli Peppers

Cibolo Junction (hot and spicy New Mexican foods)

Gourmet Cuisine (specialty gourmet dessert sauces)

Cosmopolitan Foods (Wyang brand hot chile products)

Country Bunkin's (Bubba Leroy's hot sauces)

Coyote Moon (hot sauces, salsas)

Curry House (all things curry)

CyberSauce (an extraordinary hot sauce)

Dave and Lynn's Hot Shop (200 types of hot sauce)

Dave's Special Salsa (salsa and spice)

David Beard Products (Texas salsa)

Desert Rose Foods (natural Southwestern fare)

El Paso Chile Co.

El Paso Joe's Gifts for Yankees (peppers, salsas, blankets, wall-hangings, nuts, cookbooks)

Farmer's Pick (garlic braids and chile-pepper ristras, chile-pepper decorations)

Fear Itself Seasonings

Fire Eaters (gourmet salsas, hot sauces)
FireGirl (jalapeños, habañeros, tabascos)
Fire 'n Ice Cookbook ("Mexican food with a bold new attitude!")
Flame-Boy Smoky Salsa
Foods of New Mexico
Fragrant Garden ("Plants magical, mystical, munchable, and medicinal")
Gary Products (hot sauces, condiments)
Glen's Recipe Buster (Glen Hosey's homepage— 140,000 recipes!)
Goldust Cafe at InterArt (chile, wine, recipes from the American Southwest)
Gourmet Foods of Cairo (Egyptian hot sauce; King Tut and Queen Nefertiti hot sauces)
Hacienda Flores Salsa
Harrison's Habanero Hot Sauce
Heat Me Up ("Hot as it gets!")
High Mesa Chili Salsa (Hazardous Burning Coals Salsa)
Hoosier Hot Sauce
Hot and Spicy Cuisine for Everyone
Hot and Spicy E-Zine (Judy Howle's e-zine)
Hot & Spicy Facts About Chile Peppers
Hot Hot Hot (hot sauce)
Hot 'n Stuff (salsas, spices, sauces)
Hot Pursuits (spicy, savory hot sauces)
Hot Sauce Hank's
Hot Sauce Harry's

Hot Sauces (salsas and sauces from all over the world)
Hot Shop (hot sauces, salsas, other hot stuff)
Hot Stop (hot sauces, jalapeanuts, pretzels, spices, powders)
Hotlanta ChileHead Gathering Summer '98 (for faithful chileheads and El Grande worshipers)
Hot's Desire (hot sauces, salsas, olives, mustards, barbecue sauces, spices)
House of Fire
Howlin' Hot Sauce
Huy Fong Foods (Asian hot sauces)
Iguana Hot Sauce (gourmet pepper sauces)
International Hot Foods (hot sauces, salsas, barbecue sauces, dips)
Jamacian Spices
Jane Butel's Pecos Valley Spice Company
Jardine Foods
JB's Hot Stuf (over 250 brands and kinds of hot)
Jordine Import Co. (Sontava-brand habañero pepper sauce)
Joy's (preserves and dry goods)
Judy's Taste of the South Food (spicy foods from Mississippi)
Karamba
Krista's Jamaican Jerk Sauce
La Victoria (Mexican salsas, taco sauces)
Land of Odds Gourmet Shop (Southern and Southwestern foods, hot sauces, chile, barbecue sauces, salsas)

Lawrence Wheeler's Web Pages
Le Cadeau du Terre (flavored gourmet oils and vinegars, pickled peppers, pepper jellies)
Los Chileros (chile products ranging from mild to sizzling hot)
Lotsa Hotsa (hot sauces, salsas)
Mama Scott's Gourmet Sauce (Sweet Apple to XX Picante)
Mango 'n Chili
Mark's ReMarkable Matador Processors (chile rellenos)
Melinda's Fine Food Products (salsas and sauces)
Melvin & Caryl's Hot Sauces (sauces, salsas, spices, peppers)
Mick's Peppourri (high-quality pepper jelly)
Midwest Pepper Trading Company (sauces and salsas)
Mike's World of Peppers
Mild to Wild Pepper & Herb Company (Jim Campbell's outfit)
Mo Hotta Mo Betta
Muoi Khuntilanont's Kitchen (Colonel Ian F. Khuntilanont Philpott's Thai cooking page)
Native Kjalii Foods (fire-roasted salsas, tortilla chips)
New Mexico Chile and Food Products
New Mexico Chili Pipe Line (green and red chile, ristras, chile salsas, corn products)
New Mexico Farms (farm-fresh chile peppers)
New Mexico Online Chile Source (chile products at farm-direct prices)

New Orleans Food (collection of explanations and definitions)

Off the Deep End (sauces, salsas, gourmet products)

Original Habanero Company (habañero products from Texas, hot sauces, barbecue sauces, seasonings, jellies)

Pacific Coast Outlet (hot sauces, San Diego tourist guide)

Pacific Southwest Sauces (Hawaii-based; mildly spicy products)

Panchovilla's (hot and spicy salsas)

Panola Peppers (Louisiana's finest hot sauces and spices)

Passion for Pepper Sauces

Pepper Fool (great recipes)

Pepper Island Beach (Habanero Hurricane sauce)

Pepper Joe's (chili-pepper catalog)

Pepper People (fiery gourmet foods, exotic hot sauces, unusual gifts)

Pepper Plant California-Style Hot Sauces, Salsas, and Seasonings (all-natural products)

Pepper Ranch Gourmet Hot Sauces

Pepper'ella Floribbean Jerk Sauce (jerk sauces, marinades)

Pepperman's Capsicum Carnival

Peppertown USA (PepperGirl hot sauces)

Peppers (hot sauces, peppers, seasonings, salsas, barbecue sauces)

Peppers Gourmet Fiery Foods Store, Chip's Company and Restaurant (of Dewey Beach, Delaware)

Piquant Pepper (hot and spicy chile items)

Purple Haze (habañero hot sauce)

Rattlesnake Ranch (gourmet foods from the El Paso Chile Company)

Red Fox Salsa Company (habañero salsa)

Red River of Death (elusive salsas)

Religious Experience Salsa (newsletter and recipes)

Rich McCormack's Homepage (hot foods, chiles, home-brewed beer)

Rob's Hot Foods Page (links, recipe reviews)

Rover's Salsa (salsas, spice kits)

Salsa Central! (salsa articles, recipes, news, Salsa of the Month Club)

Salsa Express

Salsa USA

Salsa Volcano (salsa kits, whole dried chiles from Mexico)

Salsas, Etc! (over 900 hot and spicy food items)

Sam McGee's Hot Gourmet (hot foods, accessories)

Satellite Mike's Souper Chili Mix

Sauce Boss (site of blues singer Bill Wharton, who makes his own hot sauce)

Seattle Soup (many kinds of soup, some with chile peppers)

Señor Mom's (chile sauce, salsas)

Shipper 'n Izzy

Singapore Unofficial Food (link to Asian foods, recipes)

Skyline Chili (restaurant chain with over 90 locations)

Smith & Smith (over 1,000 varieties of salsa, hot sauce, and horseradish)

Smokey Jo's Foods (hot sauce from Maine)

So You Like It Hot! (hot sauces, gift items for every hothead)

Sol Santa Fe Salsa (world-famous salsas by Chef Chavez of Club C)

Some Like It Hotter (sauces, salsas, coffees, snacks, spices, mustards, peppers)

Southwest Specialty Food (chiles, hot sauces, habañero products)

Southwest Spirit (catalog of gourmet salsas and hot sauces)

Standard Deviation Salsa System (create your own award-winning salsa)

Steve's Hot Sauce Page

Sungate Exotic Sauces and Suzie Hot Sauce (articles, recipes)

Tabasco (history, recipes, company store)

Talsa Salsa (exotic salsas)

Tarheel Steve's Pots, Pans, and Poetry (Steve Tanner's Web page)

Taste the Pain (hot-sauce catalog)

Thai Cooking and Travel (Thai cookbooks)

Tierra Vegetables (estate-grown and smoked chiles)

Timber's Savory Flavors (world-champion chile spices; savor those flavors)

Tombstone Prospecting Co. (sauces, seasonings, salsas)

Tres Chic of Texas (Texas hill-country outfit producing spicy salsa and jalapeño jelly)
Voodoo Chile Luke (from Australia)
Volcano Sauce
Wild Bill Hickory's Home Page
Wun-Doe-Mus (all-purpose peppery spice blend)

SEEDS

The Chile Woman
1704 South Weimer Rd.
Bloomington, IN 47403-2869
(812) 332-8494

Chris Weeks Peppers
P.O. Box 3207
Kill Devil Hills, NC 27948

The Cook's Garden
P.O. Box 5010
Hodges, SC 29653
(800) 457-9703

Cross Country Nurseries
P.O. Box 170
199 Kingwood-Locktown Rd.
Rosemont, NJ 08556-0170
(908) 996-4646; www.chileplants.com

Enchanted Seeds
P.O. Box 6087
Las Cruces, NM 88006
(505) 233-3033

High Altitude Gardens
P.O. Box 1048
Hailey, ID 83333
(208) 788-4363; www.seedsave.org

J.L. Hudson, Seedsman
P.O. Box 337
Star Rte. 2
La Honda, CA 94020

Johnny's Seeds
Foss Hill Rd.
Albion, ME 04910-9731
(207) 437-4301; www.johnnyseeds.com

Native Seeds/SEARCH
526 N. 4th Ave.
Tucson, AZ 85705
(520) 622-5561

Nichols Garden Nursery
1190 N. Pacific Highway
Albany, OR 97321
(541) 928-9280; www.gardennursery.com

The Pepper Gal
P.O. Box 23006
Fort Lauderdale, FL 33307-3006
(954) 537-5540

Pepper Joe's, Inc.
1650 Pembroke Rd.
Norristown, PA 19403
(410) 628-0507 (fax); www.pepperjoe.com

Pinetree Garden Seeds
P.O. Box 300
New Gloucester, ME 04260
(207) 926-3400; www.superseeds.com/home.htm

Plants of the Southwest
P.O. Box 11A
3095 Agua Fria Rd., Rte. 6
Santa Fe, NM 87501
(800) 788-SEED; www.plantsofthesouthwest.com/

Redwood City Seed Co.
P.O. Box 361
Redwood City, CA 94064
(650) 325-7333; www.ecoseeds.com

Santa Barbara Heirloom Seedling Nursery
P.O. Box 4235
Santa Barbara, CA 93140
(805) 968-5444

Seed Savers Exchange
3076 North Winn Rd.
Decorah, IA 52101
(319) 382-5990

Seeds of Change
P.O. Box 15700
Santa Fe, NM 87506-5700
(888) 762-7333; www.seedsofchange.com

Seeds West Garden Seeds
317 14th St. N.W.
Albuquerque, NM 87104
(505) 843-9713; www.seedswestgardenseeds.com

Shepherd's Garden Seeds
30 Irene St.
Torrington, CT 06790-6658
(860) 482-3638; www.shepherdseeds.com

Terra Time & Tide
590 E. 59th St.
Jacksonville, FL 32208
(904) 764-0376; www.pepperhot.com

Tomato Grower's Supply
P.O. Box 2237
Fort Myers, FL 33902
(941) 768-1119

Totally Tomatoes
P.O. Box 1626
Augusta, GA 30903-1626
(803) 663-0016

Tough Love Chile Co.
358–5025 S. McCarran Blvd.
Reno, NV 89502
(702) 849-3100; www.tough-love.com

Appendix 7

Mr. Chilehead's Favorite Recipes

When I first conceived of this book, I had no intention of including a recipe section. Too many of the hot-sauce books already on the market were simply compendiums of recipes. But everyone I spoke to about this project, including friends who claimed to have enjoyed the spicy fare I had cooked for them, asked, "Will there be recipes? Recipes, please!"

Given such displays of enthusiasm, Mr. Chilehead—who hates to disappoint his fellow chileheads—was obligated to respond in the affirmative. So here, for your entertainment and possible culinary pleasure, I give you some of my own all-time favorite recipes.

A number of the recipes I've selected are original Mr. Chilehead creations; others I've adapted, over time, from a range of sources, "fixing" them and making them my own. Try them—you'll like them all. Mr. Chilehead personally guarantees it.

My Father's Benchmark Hot Spaghetti Sauce

16 cups tomato juice
4 small tins tomato paste
1 celery stalk, thinly sliced
4 large onions, thinly sliced
4 large green bell peppers, thinly sliced
3 habañeros, thinly sliced
3 pounds medium ground beef
6 large garlic cloves, minced
2 tbsp. turmeric
2 tbsp. crushed red chiles
2 tbsp. curry powder
2 tbsp. cumin
2 tbsp. ground black pepper
2 tbsp. salt
Your favorite hot sauce

Heat the juice and the paste in a large pot over medium heat, stirring vigorously with a wooden spoon to blend. Add celery, onions, bell peppers, and habañeros. Stir vigorously. In a large skillet, brown the beef, breaking up any large clumps with your spoon, then add to the pot. Add the garlic and all of the spices and seasonings, except for the hot sauce. Stir vigorously. Bring mixture to a steady simmer, and add your favorite hot sauce to taste. Simmer for 3 hours.

Beef and Jalapeño Stew

2 pounds round steak, cut in 1-inch cubes
1 tbsp. flour
2 tbsp. butter
1 medium onion, chopped
2 garlic cloves, minced
4 to 6 jalapeños, seeded and finely chopped
1/2 tsp. dried oregano
1 cup tomatillo pulp or crushed tomatillo
1/2 cup water

Coat the meat with flour. Over medium heat, melt the butter in a large skillet. Add the onion and the garlic and sauté until the onion is translucent—about 5 minutes. Add the meat cubes to the pan and brown on all sides. Place meat mixture in a slow cooker and add the remaining ingredients. Cover and cook on low until the meat is very tender—6 to 8 hours.

Green Chile Stew with Irish Whiskey

1/2 cup olive oil
2 tbsp. minced garlic
2 cups Spanish onion, chopped
2 jalapeños, thinly sliced
2 tsp. salt
1 tbsp. ground black pepper
1 tbsp. dried oregano

1 pound lamb shoulder, cut in ½-inch cubes
2 ounces Irish whiskey
8 new potatoes, cut in bite-size pieces
4 cups chopped green chiles
2 medium tomatoes, chopped
8 cups beef broth

Heat the olive oil in a large, heavy stew pot. Add the garlic, onion, and jalapeños, and sauté until vegetables are just softened. Add the salt, the pepper, and the oregano, and cook the mixture for 10 more minutes. Add the lamb cubes and brown well on all sides. Add the whiskey and the potatoes and cook, stirring, for an additional 10 minutes. Mix in the green chiles and the tomatoes, and cook until all ingredients are heated through. Add the beef broth, reduce the heat, and simmer until the meat is very tender—60 to 90 minutes.

Texas Baked Beans

1 pound dried navy beans
6 ounces bacon, diced
1 large onion, chopped
1 green bell pepper, diced
1 red bell pepper, diced
1 28-ounce can of diced plum tomatoes
1/2 pound baked ham, diced
1 smoked pork chop, diced
1 cup ketchup
3/4 cup dark brown sugar

1/4 cup honey
1/4 cup dark molasses
1 tbsp. Worcestershire sauce
1 tsp. dry mustard
2 apples, peeled, cored, and cut in large dice
Salt

Rinse beans, cover them in cold water (there should be 2 inches of water over the beans), and soak over-night. Drain and rinse the beans and place them in a large saucepan. Add fresh water to cover by 2 inches, and bring to a boil. Reduce heat and simmer, skimming off any foam that rises to the surface, until the beans are just tender—about 40 minutes. Drain and set aside.

Place bacon in a large, heavy casserole pot or Dutch oven and fry over low heat until the fat is just rendered; do not brown. Remove bacon pieces from the pot with a slotted spoon and set aside. Sauté the onion in the bacon fat until softened, then add the bell peppers and stir-fry for about 5 minutes. Add the beans and the reserved bacon. Drain the tomatoes, reserving one cup of the juice, and add them to the bean mixture. Add all the remaining ingredients except the reserved tomato juice, the apples, and the salt.

Stir the mixture gently to combine, cover, and bake in a preheated 350° oven for about 2 hours. Add the tomato juice and the apples. Return the beans to the oven and bake, uncovered, until the sauce is thick and the beans are fragrant—about 2 more hours. Season with salt to taste.

Guajillo-Chicken Stew

6 dried guajillo chiles
2 pounds boneless chicken, cut in 1-inch cubes
2 tbsp. olive oil
1 large onion, chopped
3 tbsp. brown sugar
2 tsp. ground cinnamon
2 tsp. ground cloves
2 tbsp. red wine vinegar

Soak the chiles in hot water for 25 minutes to soften. Blacken the chiles over a gas burner or a grill, turning frequently. When chiles are cool enough to handle, remove stems and seeds and chop coarsely. In a deep skillet, simmer the chicken in just enough water to cover until cooked through—about 10 minutes. Remove the chicken from the cooking water, reserving the water for later use. Set aside. Wipe out the pan and heat the oil in it; add the onion and sauté until translucent. Add the brown sugar, the cinnamon, the cloves, the reserved water, and the chicken. Bring the mixture to a boil, reduce the heat, and simmer, uncovered, for 35 minutes. Stir in the vinegar, and serve.

Poblano Chicken

5 poblanos
1 cup heavy cream
Salt and pepper
3 whole boneless chicken breasts, split
1 medium onion, halved
2 garlic cloves, peeled
1/2 cup Parmesan cheese, grated
2 tbsp. butter

Roast the chiles over a grill or under a broiler, turning often to char on all sides. Place chiles in a plastic bag to steam. When they are cool enough to handle, peel them and remove the seeds and membranes. In a food processor or blender, purée the chiles with the cream and salt and pepper to taste. Strain the sauce and set aside.

Place the chicken, the onion, and the garlic in a large saucepan and cover with water. Simmer until the chicken is just cooked through—about 10 minutes.

In a greased baking dish just large enough to hold them, arrange the chicken breasts. Pour the chile sauce over them, sprinkle with the cheese, and dot with butter. Bake in a preheated 375° oven for about 20 minutes, or until the chicken is heated through and the cheese is golden.

Authentic Texas Border Chile

3 medium tomatoes
1 purple onion, finely chopped
1/4 tsp. oregano
2 tsp. paprika
5 garlic cloves, minced
3 tbsp. cumin seeds
1 tbsp. butter
4 scallions, chopped
5 green and/or red bell peppers, cut in large dice
5 serranos, julienned
1 pound sausage meat
4 pounds beef shank, coarsely ground
2 tsp. salt
4 tbsp. hot red chile powder
4 tbsp. mild red chile powder
Beer

Purée the tomatoes, the onion, the oregano, the paprika, and one clove of the garlic in a food processor fitted with a steel blade. Set aside. Toast the cumin seeds in a small skillet over medium heat for a few seconds, stirring; do not allow them to burn. Crush them in a mortar and set aside.

In a large skillet, melt the butter over medium heat. Add the scallions, the bell peppers, the serranos, the sausage meat, and the remaining garlic, and sauté, breaking up the sausage meat with a spoon, until the scallions are translucent and the meat is browned.

In a large, heavy stew pot, combine the beef, the puréed vegetables, and the pepper-sausage mixture. Add the salt and the chile powders. Pour in enough beer to cover the mixture. Bring to a boil, reduce to a simmer, and cook, uncovered, for 4 to 6 hours.

Mulato Chile

4 dried mulato chiles
1 purple onion, chopped
2 tbsp. vegetable oil
3 large garlic cloves, minced
1 tsp. chile powder
1 tsp. cinnamon
1 tbsp. cumin
1 tbsp. dried oregano
1 tsp. salt
2 28-ounce cans stewed tomatoes
1 1/2 cups black beans, presoaked and cooked
2 tsp. unsweetened cocoa powder
Tomato juice

Soak the chiles in hot water for 25 minutes, or until they soften. Sauté the onion in the oil until translucent. Add the garlic, chile powder, cinnamon, cumin, oregano, and salt, along with the tomatoes. Bring to a boil, reduce to a simmer, and cook for 25 minutes. Add the black beans and the cocoa powder and mix well. Thin the chile with the tomato juice until it reaches the desired consistency, and heat through before serving.

Jalapeño Poppers

8 ounces cream cheese, softened
4 ounces old Cheddar cheese, grated
4 ounces Monterey Jack cheese, grated
6 bacon slices, cooked and coarsely chopped
1/4 tsp. chile powder
1/4 tsp. garlic powder
1 pound jalapeños, halved lengthwise and seeded
1/2 cup dry bread crumbs

Preheat oven to 300°. In a bowl, combine cheeses, bacon, and seasonings, blending well. Fill each jalapeño half with about two tablespoons of the mixture. Roll the pepper halves in breadcrumbs and arrange them on a greased baking sheet. Bake according to your preferred level of spiciness: 20 minutes for hot; 30 minutes for medium; and 40 minutes for mild.

Serve with sour cream or your favorite dip.

Red Pepper Pâté

4 large red bell peppers
3 garlic cloves, unpeeled
2 tbsp. balsamic vinegar
1 tbsp. sweet chile sauce
12 tbsp. (1 1/2 sticks) butter, melted
Sugar
2 tsp. parsley, finely chopped

Preheat oven to 475°. Line a baking sheet with foil. Quarter the peppers lengthwise and remove the seeds and membranes. Arrange peppers on the baking sheet with the garlic and roast for 20 minutes. Place peppers in a plastic bag to steam. When they are cool enough to handle, peel them and the garlic cloves.

In a food processor, purée the peppers and the garlic with the vinegar and the chile sauce. Leave the motor running and pour in the melted butter in a thin, steady stream. Continue processing until the mixture is thick and creamy.

Transfer the mixture to a small saucepan, and cook over low heat for 15 minutes, stirring often. Remove from heat and stir in a pinch of sugar and the parsley. Chill pâté until it is set—at least 3 hours.

Serve the pâté with crackers, or use it as a pizza or pasta sauce.

Flaming Coleslaw

Slaw:
8 ounces cabbage, finely shredded
1 garlic clove, minced
1/4 cup minced Bermuda onion
3 jalapeños, julienned

Dressing:
1/2 tsp. fresh oregano, minced
1/2 tsp. sesame chile oil

1 tsp. brown sugar
1/4 cup rice wine vinegar
1/2 cup water

Mix the slaw ingredients together in a large bowl. Whisk the dressing ingredients together in a smaller bowl. Toss slaw with the dressing. Cover the coleslaw and refrigerate for at least 4 hours, or overnight. Serve well chilled.

Jalapeño Brownies

2/3 cup semisweet chocolate chips
1/2 cup butter
4 large eggs
1/2 tsp. salt
2 cups sugar
1 tsp. vanilla
1 1/4 cups flour
1/4 cup unsweetened cocoa powder
5 large jalapeños, minced
6 to 8 tiny Thai chiles, minced
3/4 cup walnuts, toasted and chopped

Preheat oven to 350°. Melt butter and chocolate chips together in the top of a double boiler. Set aside to cool. In a large bowl, beat the eggs with the salt until foamy.

Add the sugar and the vanilla, and beat until well blended. Add the chocolate-butter mixture and stir until just combined, then add the flour and the cocoa powder and mix until almost blended. Fold in the jalapeños, the chiles, and the nuts. Pour mixture into a greased 9- x 13-inch pan, and bake until the top forms a cracked crust and the inside looks slightly moist—25 to 30 minutes. When brownies have cooled, shake powdered sugar over top and cut in squares.

Habañero-Lime Cheesecake

Crust:
1/2 cup graham cracker crumbs
Melted butter

Filling:
3 habañeros
2 tbsp. sugar
24 ounces cream cheese, softened
1 cup sugar
1/4 tsp. salt
4 large eggs
2 tbsp. heavy cream
Zest of 1 lime
Juice of 2 limes
1 lime, thinly sliced, for garnish

Adjust oven racks so that there is one in the middle and another below it, and preheat oven to 400°. Make the filling by mixing the graham cracker crumbs with butter, adding the butter gradually until the crumbs just hold together. Set aside ¼ cup of this mixture and press the rest into the bottom and up the sides of a 9-inch springform pan.

Roast the habañeros over a grill or under a broiler, turning frequently to char evenly. Put them in a plastic bag to steam; when they are cool enough to handle, peel and seed them. Pound the habañeros with the 2 tbsp. of sugar in a mortar, or pulse in a food processor, until they are reduced to a coarse paste.

Cream the cream cheese with the cup of sugar and the salt. Beat in the eggs, one at a time, then beat in the cream. Add the lime zest and juice, and stir until well incorporated. Add the habañero paste and mix thoroughly. Pour the filling into the crust and sprinkle the reserved crumbs over the top.

Fill a baking pan with boiling water and place it on the oven's lower rack. Place the cheesecake on the rack above it and bake until the cake pulls away from the sides of the pan—about one hour. Allow the cake to set for about 20 minutes, then release and remove pan. Wrap the cake in plastic wrap and freeze for three hours, or refrigerate overnight. Before serving, garnish with lime slices.

Ginger-Orange Custard

4 large eggs
1 ¾ cups superfine sugar
2 tbsp. orange liqueur
1 tbsp. fresh ginger, finely chopped
3 serranos, seeded and diced
4 cups double cream

Whisk the eggs and the sugar together in the top of a double boiler, then add the liqueur, the ginger, the serranos, and the cream. Bring the boiler to a simmer and cook the mixture, stirring constantly, until it thickens—about 30 minutes. Pour the custard into serving dishes and chill until firm—about 2 hours.

Macadamia-Almond Brittle

1 cup sugar
1/2 cup light corn syrup
3/4 cup macadamia nuts, coarsely chopped
3/4 cup almonds, coarsely chopped
1/4 tsp. habañero powder
1 tsp. butter
2 tbsp. vanilla
1 tsp. baking soda

In a 1-quart microwave-safe dish, mix together the sugar and the corn syrup. Microwave on high for 5 minutes, then mix in the nuts and the habañero powder. Microwave for another 4 minutes, or until a candy themometer registers 302° (the hard-crack stage). Working quickly, add the butter, the vanilla, and the baking soda, stirring until the mixture is light and foamy. When the bubbles subside, pour the mixture onto a greased baking sheet, and, using a metal spatula, spread it as thinly as possible. Allow the mixture to cool completely, then break it into small pieces.

Store in a airtight container with waxed paper between the layers.

Tomatillo Salsa

- 4 large ancho chiles
- 6 large garlic cloves, unpeeled
- 1 celery stalk, diced
- 15 tomatillos, diced
- 2 medium tomatoes, diced
- 1 large white onion, diced
- 1 tbsp. vinegar
- Juice of 2 limes
- 1 small bunch cilantro, coarse stems removed, chopped

Preheat oven to 400°. Roast the ancho chiles and the garlic until the chiles are puffed and the garlic is soft. Set aside to cool. Combine celery, tomatillos, tomatoes, and onion in a glass or ceramic bowl. Add the vinegar and the lime juice. Remove the garlic from its skin, mash, and add to the bowl, along with the cilantro. Crumble the roasted ancho chiles into the mixture. Mix the salsa well, cover, and refrigerate for several hours before serving.

Chile de Árbol Salsa

- 1 ounce dried de árbol chiles (about 40), stemmed and seeded
- 1 large garlic clove, unpeeled
- 2 Roma tomatoes
- 1/4 tsp. cumin seeds
- 1/4 tsp. fresh oregano
- 1/4 tsp. salt

In a frying pan, stir the chiles over medium heat until well toasted. Soak chiles in a quart of warm water for about 40 minutes to rehydrate. Drain chiles, reserving one cup of the soaking liquid, and set aside. Roast the garlic in a hot oven until very soft. Blacken the tomatoes over a grill or under the broiler. Peel garlic and tomatoes and set aside. Toast the cumin seeds and the oregano over medium heat for a few seconds, stirring, until fragrant; do not allow the mixture to burn. In a spice grinder or mortar, grind cumin seeds and oregano to a powder. Transfer all ingredients, including salt, to a food processor or blender, and purée. Mix salsa well, cover, and refrigerate for several hours before serving.

Mango–Scotch Bonnet Salsa

1 large ripe mango, peeled, pitted, and diced
1/4 cup minced purple onion
1/2 a Scotch bonnet, seeded and minced
Juice of 1 large lime
2 tbsp. cilantro, chopped
1/2 tsp. cumin
1/2 tsp. salt
1/4 tsp. ground white pepper

Combine all of the ingredients in a bowl and mix well. Refrigerate the salsa for at least 1 hour before serving.

Bottled Hell Sauce

2 cups fresh or dried datil peppers, stems removed, chopped
3 cups white vinegar
8 cups ketchup

Blend the peppers and 1/2 cup of the vinegar in a blender until smooth. Pour the mixture into a large saucepan, and stir in the remaining vinegar and the ketchup. Bring to a boil, reduce the heat, and simmer for 10 minutes. Cool slightly and pour into clean glass bottles or jars. Cap securely. Refrigerate for one week before serving.

New Mexico Red Chile Sauce

10 to 12 dried red New Mexican chiles, stemmed and seeded
3 cups water
2 tbsp. vegetable oil
1 medium onion, chopped
2 garlic cloves, chopped

Rinse the chiles and place them in a medium saucepan with the water. Bring to a boil, reduce the heat, and simmer for 15 to 20 minutes. Sauté the onion and the garlic in the oil until the onion is translucent. Place all the ingredients, including the chile water, in a food processor or blender and purée until smooth. For a smooth sauce, strain before serving.

Malaysian Chile Paste

2 tbsp. fresh ginger, finely chopped
4 lemon grass stalks, tough outer layers removed, finely chopped
4 garlic cloves, minced
1/4 cup unsalted peanuts, chopped
6 shallots, finely chopped
40 Thai red chiles, seeded and chopped
1 tsp. black peppercorns, crushed
1 tsp. palm sugar
1 tsp. turmeric
3 tsp. salt

Grind all of the ingredients in a food processor until reduced to a smooth paste.

Pepperoncini Martinis

1 ounce dry white vermouth
16 ounces vodka
4 pickled pepperoncinis

Fill a cocktail shaker with ice. Add the vermouth and the vodka and stir gently. Place one pepper in each of 4 large martini glasses, and strain the martini mixture equally into each glass.

References

Andrews, Jean. *Peppers: The Domesticated Capsicums*. Austin: U of Texas Press, 1984.

Anonymous. "No Pain, No Gain." *Chile Peppers: A Chilehead's Manual for the New Millennium*. N.p., n.d.

DeWitt, Dave, and Nancy Gerlach. *The Whole Chile Pepper Book*. Boston: Little, Brown, 1990.

Evans, Chuck, and Dave DeWitt. *The Hot Sauce Bible*. Freedom, CA: Crossing Press, 1996.

Jackson, David G. "Peppered Personalities: A Continuing Series." www.fiery-foods.com/zine-industry

Kloss, Jethro. *Back to Eden*. Santa Barbara: Woodbridge, 1985.

Naj, Amal. *Peppers: A Story of Hot Pursuits*. New York: Knopf, 1992.

Pinkwater, Daniel. "A Hot Time in Nairobi." *Hoboken Fish and Chicago Whistle*. Xlibris: 1999.

Roeder, Beatrice. *Chicano Folk Medicine from Los Angeles, California*. Berkeley: U of California Press, 1988.

Thompson, Jennifer Trainer. *Hot Licks: Great Recipes for Making and Cooking with Hot Sauces*. San Francisco: Chronicle, 1994.

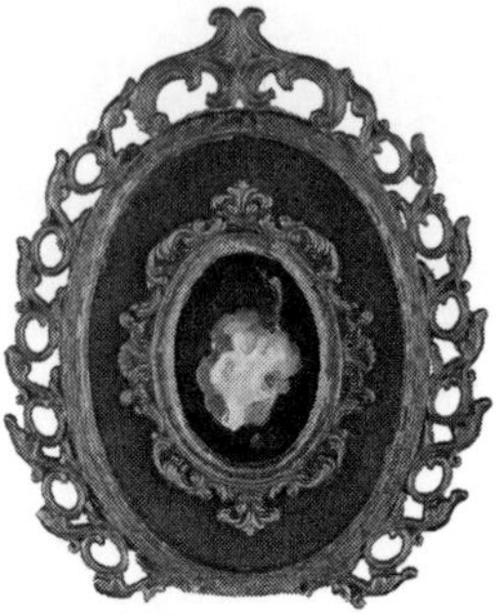